THE LIZZIE BORDEN AX MURDERS

BY CARLA MOONEY

CONTENT CONSULTANT
ANNETTE M. HOLBA
PROFESSOR OF RHETORIC
PLYMOUTH STATE UNIVERSITY

AMERICAN CRIME STORIES

An Imprint of Abdo Publishing | abdobooks.com

ABDOBOOKS.COM

Published by Abdo Publishing, a division of ABDO, PO Box 398166, Minneapolis, Minnesota 55439.

Printed in the United States of America, North Mankato, Minnesota.
102019
012020

Cover Photo: AP Images
Interior Photos: Donna Hageman/Chicago Tribune/Tribune News Service/Getty Images, 5; Bettmann/Getty Images, 8, 10, 17, 20 (top), 20 (bottom left), 20 (bottom middle); Granger Historical Picture Archive, 15; AP Images, 20 (bottom right), 65; Bill Greene/Boston Globe/Getty Images, 23; Charles Krupa/AP Images, 24; Everett Collection/Newscom, 30; Carl Nesensohn/AP Images, 33; The Picture Art Collection/Alamy, 38–39; Smith Collection/Gado/Archive Photos/Getty Images, 43; Pictures Now/Alamy, 45; Franck Fotos/Alamy, 50; Cindy Hopkins/Alamy, 53; crossroadscreative/iStockphoto, 56; Frank Middendorf/Shutterstock Images, 60; Steven Senne/AP Images, 70; Everett Collection Historical/Alamy, 73; Classic Images/ Alamy, 77; The History Collection/Alamy, 78–79; Red Line Editorial, 82; Bert Lane/AP Images, 86; Lisa Poole/AP Images, 89; Matt Rourke/AP Images, 91; Pat Greenhouse/ Boston Globe/Getty Images, 95; Jonathan Wiggs/The Boston Globe/Getty Images, 96–97

Editor: Charly Haley
Series Designer: Melissa Martin

LIBRARY OF CONGRESS CONTROL NUMBER: 2019941920

PUBLISHER'S CATALOGING-IN-PUBLICATION DATA

Names: Mooney, Carla, author.
Title: The Lizzie Borden ax murders/ by Carla Mooney
Description: Minneapolis, Minnesota: Abdo Publishing, 2020 | Series: American crime stories | Includes online resources and index.
Identifiers: ISBN 9781532190100 (lib. bdg) | ISBN 9781532175954 (ebook)
Subjects: LCSH: Borden, Lizzie, 1860-1927--Juvenile literature. | Killing (Murder)--Juvenile literature. | Parricide--Juvenile literature. | Trials (Murder)--Massachusetts--Juvenile literature. | Homicide--Juvenile literature.
Classification: DDC 364.152--dc23

CONTENTS

CHAPTER ONE

A HORRIFYING CRIME

The morning of Thursday, August 4, 1892, began like any other summer day in Fall River, Massachusetts. At the Borden home on Second Street, Andrew Jackson Borden and his wife, Abby, ate breakfast. Borden was one of the wealthiest men in Fall River. They were joined in the dining room by John Vinnicum Morse, Borden's brother-in-law by his late first wife. Morse had arrived in Fall River the previous day and had spent the night at the Borden home. Around 9:00 a.m., the two men left for business in the city, headed in opposite directions.

Abby Borden busied herself with household chores. She instructed Bridget "Maggie" Sullivan, the Bordens' housemaid, to wash the first-floor windows. Mrs. Borden then climbed the stairs to the second floor. She planned to straighten up the guest room where Morse had slept the night before.

The Borden house still stands in Fall River, Massachusetts, and it is open to visitors.

Lizzie Borden

Thirty-two-year-old Lizzie Andrew Borden, Andrew Borden's youngest daughter, came downstairs later than her father, stepmother, and uncle. She ate breakfast alone in the dining room. Her older sister, Emma Borden, also lived at the family home but was away visiting a friend in Fairhaven, Massachusetts.

Around 10:30 a.m., Andrew Borden returned home from downtown earlier than he had planned. He had completed his morning business errands at the bank, a meeting with a commercial tenant, and a visit to the barbershop. Feeling slightly under the weather, he went into the first-floor sitting room and lay down on the couch. Finished with the outside windows, Sullivan began to wash the inside windows. Lizzie went into the dining room to iron her handkerchiefs.

A VISITOR ARRIVES

The night before the murders, John Vinnicum Morse arrived at the Borden house for a visit. Morse was the brother of Sarah Morse Borden, Mr. Borden's first wife. When he was about 20 years old, Morse left Massachusetts and traveled west. Eventually, he settled in Iowa and became a successful horse trader. Each summer, he traveled back to Massachusetts and visited Fall River and New Bedford. Andrew Borden and John Morse were friendly and often discussed business matters.

Tragedy Discovered

After washing the windows, Sullivan went to her third-floor room to rest on the bed for a few minutes. At about 11:00 a.m., she heard Lizzie yelling for her to come quickly. Sullivan asked what was wrong. Lizzie replied, "Come down quick; Father's dead; somebody came in and killed him."[1] Sullivan ran down the back stairs of the Borden home. As she turned toward the sitting room, Lizzie warned her, "Oh, Maggie, don't go in. I have got to have a doctor quick. Go over. I have got to have the doctor."[2]

Sullivan ran to the home of Dr. Seabury Bowen, but he was not home. She left a message with his wife and returned to the Borden home. Lizzie ordered her to get Alice Russell, a friend who lived a few blocks away. Sullivan rushed off again.

Meanwhile, Adelaide Churchill, who lived next door to the Bordens, noticed Sullivan's frantic rushing back and forth. She called out her window to Lizzie and asked if anything was wrong. Lizzie called her over and told her that someone had killed her father. Churchill asked Lizzie where

BRIDGET SULLIVAN

Bridget Sullivan, the Bordens' housemaid, was an immigrant from Ireland. At the time of the murders, she was 26 years old and had been working for the Bordens for almost three years. Although her first name was Bridget, the Bordens often called her "Maggie," the name of a former housemaid. Sullivan's duties included ironing, cooking, and cleaning. She was not responsible for cleaning any of the bedrooms except her own, as the Borden sisters and Mrs. Borden cleaned their own rooms. Not long after the 1892 murders, Sullivan left Fall River and eventually settled in Montana, where she worked as a housemaid.

her stepmother was. Lizzie replied that her stepmother had received a note earlier that morning and had gone out to visit a sick friend. Churchill also asked Lizzie where she was when her father was attacked. Lizzie replied that she had gone to the barn to get a piece of iron. She worried that someone was out to kill her entire family, saying, "Father must have an enemy, for we have all been sick, and we think the milk has been poisoned. . . . Dr. Bowen is not at home, and I must have a doctor."[3] Churchill reassured Lizzie that she would find a doctor. She left the Borden home and hurried to a nearby stable where she asked a man to get a doctor and notify the police. Then she returned to the Borden home. Soon Sullivan returned, and Dr. Bowen arrived.

Andrew Borden was 70 years old when he died.

A Gruesome Scene

Bowen entered the sitting room to examine Andrew Borden. He was shocked at the horrific scene. Mr. Borden lay on the lounge. His face was badly cut and covered with blood. He was barely recognizable. From the size of the wounds, the doctor believed that Mr. Borden had been cut by a sharp object such as a hatchet or an ax. Bowen felt for Mr. Borden's pulse and found none. He glanced around the room, noting that nothing appeared out of place or disturbed. He went back to the kitchen and asked Sullivan to get a sheet to cover up the body. Lizzie asked the doctor to telegraph her sister Emma to ask her to come home immediately.

Around 11:20 a.m., Officer George Allen arrived at the Borden home to check on the reported disturbance. He examined Mr. Borden's body and then left the house to get more police officers. Meanwhile, no one had heard from or seen Abby Borden. Lizzie asked the people who had gathered in the house to look for her stepmother. Afraid that a killer still lurked in the house, Sullivan and Churchill went upstairs together in search of Mrs. Borden. On the second floor, the two women discovered Mrs. Borden's body on the floor in the guest room, next to the bed. It was about 11:30 a.m. The room itself was in perfect order; nothing had been taken. The two women rushed downstairs to the dining room where Lizzie was waiting with

Russell, who had arrived moments earlier. “Is there another?” Russell asked. “Yes, she is up there,” Churchill replied.[4]

When Bowen returned from the telegraph office, Churchill told him that they had found Mrs. Borden’s body. Bowen went upstairs to the guest room. He found that Mrs. Borden had no pulse. He also noticed that she had the same type of wounds as Mr. Borden and concluded that she had been killed by the same weapon. Her body was cold, indicating that she had been killed before her husband.

Abby Borden was 64 when she died.

DESCRIBING THE SCENE

On August 4, 1892, a reporter for the *Fall River Herald* entered the Borden house. He described the terrible sight at the crime scene in the newspaper's August 4, 1892, afternoon edition. He wrote:

> *On the lounge in the cozy sitting room on the first floor of the building lay Andrew J. Borden, dead. His face presented a sickening sight. Over the left temple, a wound six by four had been made as if the head had been pounded with the dull edge of an axe. The left eye had been dug out, and a cut extended the length of the nose. The face was hacked to pieces, and the blood had covered the man's shirt and soaked into his clothing. Everything about the room was in order, and there were no signs of a scuffle of any kind.*[5]

Examining the Crime Scene

Throughout the afternoon, dozens of policemen arrived at the Borden home. Reporters and curious neighbors also wandered onto the property. As the Borden family was wealthy and well-known in the community, the police proceeded cautiously. They searched the house for any clues to the murder. They found nothing with blood on it, and the killer did not leave a weapon near the bodies.

The day of the murders, the police found no sign of forced entry into the Borden home even though the family regularly locked the doors.

Dr. William Dolan, the county's medical examiner, checked both bodies and concluded that Mrs. Borden had been killed more than an hour before her husband. Additionally, whoever had killed Mr. Borden had left money in his wallet, which made it unlikely that the motive for the murder was robbery. Officers also searched the house for the note calling Mrs. Borden to visit a sick friend, but they couldn't find it.

A Cool Manner

In the hours after the discovery of the bodies, police interviewed everyone in the house. When Assistant Marshal John Fleet interrogated Lizzie, she appeared calm and detached. When he asked her where she was at the time of the murder, Lizzie said she had gone to the barn to look for some lead or iron to use as sinkers with her fishing poles, as she had an upcoming fishing trip with friends. She lingered in the barn loft, eating a pear from the backyard tree. When she went back inside, she found her father's body.

Although Lizzie claimed to be in the house at the time of her stepmother's murder, she said she did not hear any noises even when Mrs. Borden, who was a large woman, fell to the floor.

At one point during the interview, Fleet called Abby Borden her mother. Lizzie corrected him immediately. "She is not my mother, sir; she is my stepmother," she said.[6] Although true, the way Lizzie spoke struck him as cold. He also noted that it was unusual that Lizzie never shed a tear the entire day.

THE BORDEN FUNERAL

On Saturday, August 6, 1892, Emma and Lizzie Borden held a private funeral in their home on Second Street for Andrew and Abby Borden. About 75 invited guests attended the private funeral. Black cloth draped the silver-handled caskets. The caskets were open to show the bodies of Mr. and Mrs. Borden. Mr. Borden's casket was decorated with an ivy wreath, while Mrs. Borden's was adorned with a bouquet of white roses, ferns, and pea blossoms held together by a white satin ribbon. The simple service lasted about 25 minutes and included readings and prayers. No eulogy or personal remarks were given. Outside the Borden home, more than 2,000 people packed the street to catch a glimpse of the mourners as they left the house to board carriages to the private burial.[8]

Officer Phillip Harrington also felt Lizzie was unusually calm that day, given the circumstances. He wrote about her behavior:

> *There was not the least indication of agitation, no sign of sorrow or grief, no lamentation of the heart, no comment on the horror of the crime, and no expression of a wish that the criminal be caught. All this, and something that, to me, is indescribable, gave birth to a thought that was most revolting. I thought, at least, she knew more than she wished to tell.*[7]

Word spread quickly through the Fall River community that Andrew and Abby Borden had been murdered in their own home in the middle of the day. The *Fall River Herald* newspaper, which had already released that day's paper when the murders occurred, released a second special edition that afternoon to spread the news about the horrific crime. Hundreds of people gathered on Second Street, anxiously waiting for more information. They feared that a killer was loose in the community. No one felt safe.

CHAPTER TWO

A WELL-KNOWN FAMILY

The Borden family was well-known in the Fall River community. Generations of Bordens had lived in New England for many years. No one expected the family to be involved in such a horrific crime.

Andrew Borden's Success

Andrew Borden was a wealthy man. He was not born into his position but instead earned his success. The son of a laborer, Borden was driven to make more of himself. He worked as a carpenter and cabinetmaker, and he ran a furniture business. In addition to selling furniture, Borden's business sold burial cases and coffins. Borden also invested in real estate and textile mills, and he served on the boards of several banks. By the time of his death in 1892, Borden's smart business sense helped him accumulate a fortune worth more than $250,000.[1] Today, this would be worth nearly $7 million.

Lizzie Borden's middle name was Andrew, after her father.

FALL RIVER IN THE 1890S

In the 1890s, Fall River was a typical New England mill town. It was the hub of cotton textile production in the United States, with more than 100 mills.[2] The city owed its successful mills and its name to the Quequechan River's waterfalls. Numerous mills and factories lined the river's banks. They were powered by the falls. The mills employed thousands of immigrant workers, many of whom were from Ireland.

In 1845, Borden married Sarah Anthony Morse, a seamstress and the daughter of a farmer. They had three daughters, Emma (born in 1851), Alice (1856), and Lizzie (1860). Borden's second daughter, Alice, died in 1858, just before her second birthday. In 1863, tragedy struck the family again as Sarah Morse Borden died. Her death left Andrew Borden a widower with a two-year-old and 12-year-old daughter to raise.

Abby Borden

In 1865, Borden married 37-year-old Abby Durfee Gray. Some people believed that Andrew Borden married her because he needed someone to look after his home and daughters. The girls were young when Abby Borden became their stepmother, but their relationship with

In 1890, Fall River was the fortieth-largest urban area in the United States with a population of 74,398.[3]

her was never close. Teenager Emma referred to her stepmother by her first name and never called her "Mother." Lizzie was also reserved around her stepmother, preferring to confide in her older sister instead.

Although Mrs. Borden was not close with her stepdaughters, she was close with her younger half-sister Sarah Whitehead. When Sarah and her husband faced losing their home, Abby Borden convinced her husband to buy the property in her name. The Bordens then allowed the Whiteheads to live at the property rent-free. Emma and Lizzie objected to the purchase of the home for Mrs. Borden's sister.

Emma Borden, *right*, promised her mother, Sarah Morse Borden, that she would look after young Lizzie.

CHARITABLE WORKS

Unmarried at age 32, Lizzie Borden spent her time in various charitable works. In the 1890s, this was one of the only culturally accepted activities outside the home for women of her class. Some people believe that Lizzie hoped her charitable activities would also improve her social position in town. She volunteered to teach Chinese immigrant children at Sunday school for the town's society church, the Central Congregational Church. Lizzie also served as the secretary-treasurer of the local Christian Endeavor Society, was a member of the Women's Christian Temperance Union, and did a little work for the Ladies Fruit and Flower Mission.

They saw it as proof that their father favored his wife over his daughters. To appease his daughters, Mr. Borden purchased another house for them to use as an investment property. However, the girls eventually lost interest in the house and returned it to their father.

Following the arguments about purchasing the Whitehead home, tensions were high in the Borden house. Emma and Lizzie refused to eat with their father and stepmother, so the housemaid, Bridget Sullivan, was forced to serve two sittings for each meal. The girls also refused to speak to Mrs. Borden except to answer a direct question. Lizzie made a point of referring to Mrs. Borden as her stepmother. In March 1892, Lizzie corrected her dressmaker for calling Mrs. Borden her mother. "Don't say that to me, for she is a mean good-for-nothing," Lizzie said.[4]

A Frugal Man

Andrew Borden's frugal habits were another source of tension in the Borden household. Mr. Borden insisted on remaining in the house on Second Street. Although he could have afforded a more expensive home, he liked the Second Street house because it was close to the town's business district. His daughters would have preferred to move to the Hill, where many of Fall River's elite society lived.

Life in the Second Street house was simple because Mr. Borden preferred it that way. The Borden house lacked several modern conveniences that many middle-class families enjoyed. Yet, although he was frugal, Mr. Borden had a soft spot for his youngest daughter, Lizzie. In 1890, he sent Lizzie on a grand tour of Europe with several friends. From time to time, he also bought Lizzie expensive gifts, such as a sealskin cape and a diamond ring. Lizzie returned her father's affections. She gave him a thin gold ring that he wore on his finger until his death.

A SECURE HOUSE

The Borden house had a series of locks to prevent intruders. The front door was always kept triple-locked, while the other doors to outside were also locked. Upstairs, the house had no central halls. The upstairs bedrooms opened into each other. Andrew and Abby Borden locked the door that opened from their room into Lizzie's room, while Lizzie moved furniture to block her side of the connecting door. Andrew Borden also locked the other door to his bedroom every day.

BORDEN FAMILY TREE

Sarah Morse Borden
(1823–1863)

Andrew Borden
(1822–1892)

Abby Borden
(1828–1892)

(married 1845–1863)

(married 1865–1892)

Emma Borden
(1851–1927)

Alice Borden
(1856–1858)

Lizzie Borden
(1860–1927)

Spoiled Fish or Poison?

On August 2, 1892, the Bordens ate leftover swordfish for dinner. In the late 1800s, there were no modern refrigerators. In the heat of summer, food often spoiled. That evening and into the next day, Mr. and Mrs. Borden, Lizzie, and Sullivan all complained of stomach pains and nausea.

Although stomach trouble from spoiled food was common in Fall River during the summer months, Mrs. Borden suspected something more sinister. She was convinced that she had been poisoned. On August 3, she visited her doctor and confided her suspicions to him. After learning that she had eaten fish at dinner, the doctor dismissed her concerns and blamed the spoiled fish.

On August 3, Lizzie visited her friend Alice Russell. Lizzie confided in Russell, saying that she, too, suspected the family had been poisoned. Lizzie also mentioned that her father had received some vague threats from unnamed men. She feared someone was trying to harm her family. Russell reassured her friend that no one meant the Bordens any harm. Less than 24 hours later, Andrew and Abby Borden would be hacked to death in their own home.

CHAPTER THREE

THE INVESTIGATION

After the brutal murders were discovered, the Fall River Police Department launched an investigation. With the exception of the victims' bodies, there were no signs of any disturbance throughout the Borden home. Police officers could not find the weapon. At first, no one reported hearing or seeing anything strange around the time of the murders, even though the home was on a busy street near the center of town.

Searching for Evidence

The police searched the Borden home for any clues that might have helped identify the killer. Assistant Marshal John Fleet created a timeline of the morning of the murders. He estimated that Abby Borden was killed first, around 9:30 a.m. Around 10:45 a.m., Andrew Borden returned home and settled on the sofa for a late-morning nap. Sometime between 10:45 a.m. and a little after 11:00 a.m., Mr. Borden was killed, according to Fleet.

A copy of the *Fall River Herald* newspaper shows how the Borden murders shook the town.

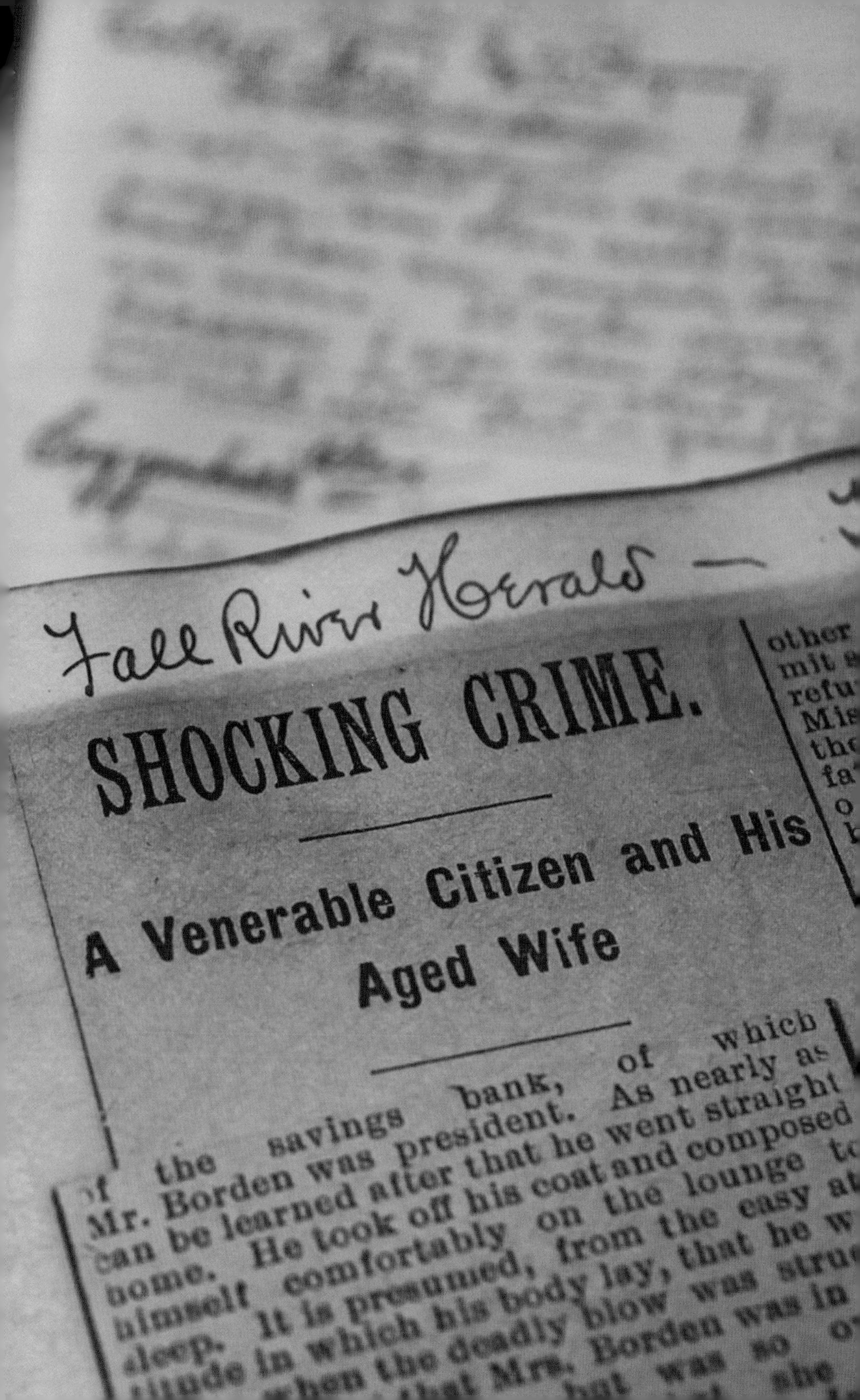

Fall River Herald —

SHOCKING CRIME.

A Venerable Citizen and His Aged Wife

of the savings bank, of which Mr. Borden was president. As nearly as can be learned after that he went straight home. He took off his coat and composed himself comfortably on the lounge to sleep. It is presumed, from the easy attitude in which his body lay, that he w[as] ... when the deadly blow was struck ... that Mrs. Borden was in ...

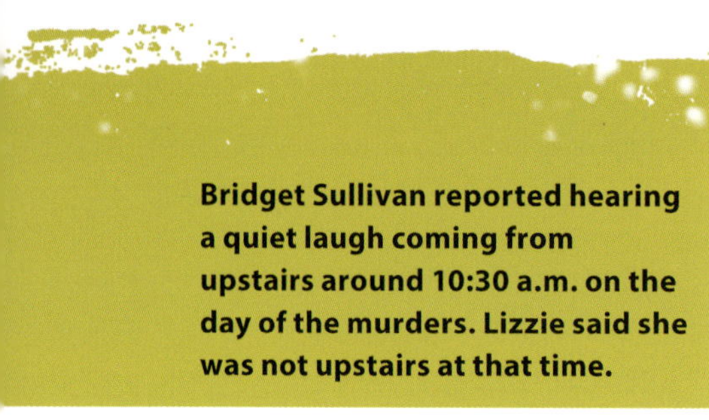

Bridget Sullivan reported hearing a quiet laugh coming from upstairs around 10:30 a.m. on the day of the murders. Lizzie said she was not upstairs at that time.

This timeline highlighted a difficult question—how did the killer manage to murder both Bordens without Lizzie or Sullivan hearing something? There was nearly an hour and a half between the two murders. The killer would have had to remain hidden from both Lizzie and Sullivan during that time.

Because it appeared both victims had been struck with an ax or hatchet, the police searched for these items. Sullivan led several police officers including Fleet down to the basement. There, they found several axes and hatchets. One hatchet head found in a box had a freshly broken handle and was not covered in dust like the other items in the box. Instead, it appeared to have ashes on both sides. Another ax had

Police found this hatchet with a broken handle in the Borden home, among other axes and hatchets. They confiscated these as evidence.

gray hairs stuck to it. The officers took the axes and hatchets as evidence.

As police searched the Borden home, they also took photos of the crime scene. This was one of the first cases in the history of US law enforcement that used crime scene photography as part of the investigation. Today, it is standard procedure for police to photograph crime scenes as part of their investigations.

The police overlooked some things in their examination of the Borden crime scene. No one asked to examine Lizzie's or Sullivan's clothing for blood or other evidence. In addition, the technique of fingerprinting to identify a criminal, which was new at the time, was not performed at the Borden murder scene because fingerprinting was not yet used by the Fall River Police Department. As they searched for clues, the police also wondered about the Bordens. Why would anyone want to so brutally attack and kill them?

Police Interviews

As part of their investigation in the hours and days after the murders, police interviewed family, friends, and townspeople. Rumors swirled that one of the immigrant workers employed by the Bordens had been at the house that morning demanding money. Police questioned immigrant laborers in town, but the lead proved to be a dead end. Another person reported

ORIGINS OF FINGERPRINTING

Every fingerprint is unique. All people have their own patterns of swirls and loops on their fingertips. As a result, fingerprints can be used to identify a person. In 1880, physician Henry Faulds published a paper that suggested that fingerprints left at a crime scene could be used to identify criminals. His idea was mainly ignored until in 1892, when Sir Francis Galton created the first fingerprint classification system based on the patterns of arches and loops found in fingerprints. Law enforcement officers around the world began experimenting with this idea as well, eventually developing a fingerprinting system that could be used for police analysis. In 1892, Francisca Rojas, who killed her two children in Argentina, became the first person in the world to be convicted based on fingerprint evidence.

seeing a pale young man walking nervously on Second Street the morning of the murders. Police identified the man and ruled him out as the killer as well. Other reports of suspicious strangers were investigated but yielded no concrete evidence. "I have devoted attention to many stories that were foolish just because of the enormity of the crime, and in order that I might leave no stone unturned to solve it," explained Marshal Rufus Hilliard.[1]

Given the fear of poisoning that both Mrs. Borden and Lizzie had recently expressed, police also questioned local pharmacies to see if anyone had recently bought poison. Pharmacist Eli Bence told them a troubling story. On August 3, a woman entered D. R. Smith's drugstore where Bence worked. She attempted to buy prussic acid. Prussic acid is a colorless liquid that is also a quick-acting poison. The woman, whom

Bence identified as Lizzie Borden, explained that she planned to use the prussic acid to clean a sealskin cape. Bence refused to sell her the prussic acid without a doctor's prescription.

Suspicions in Town

As the police investigated, people and journalists in Fall River puzzled over the crime. They wondered who could have committed such an offense and for what motive. How had the murderer managed to pull off the killings without being seen or heard by anyone? Everyone came up with their own theories to explain the murder.

Some in town suspected John Morse was involved. He was an outsider who conveniently arrived in town the night before the murders. One newspaper even called Morse "The Suspected Man."[2] Like Andrew Borden, Morse was very reserved, to the point where many people who met him

WOMEN IN THE NINETEENTH CENTURY

In 1892, many people hesitated to believe that a woman like Lizzie Borden could have possibly committed such brutal murders. Compared with men, women rarely commit murder. In the nineteenth century, the crime was even more uncommon among upper-class women like Lizzie. At the time, women were thought to be fragile and delicate. They were expected to marry and devote their lives to raising children and taking care of the home. Those who did not marry were expected to do charity work and then retire to their homes where they lived with their parents, as Lizzie did. In her 30s, Lizzie was well past the traditional marrying age.

thought he was peculiar. In the days after the murders, an angry mob of townspeople followed him around until police stopped them. However, Morse appeared to have an alibi. At the time of Andrew Borden's murder, Morse was riding a streetcar. Additionally, the relatives that he visited the morning of the murders confirmed that he was with them.

Others were convinced that Sullivan was guilty. Dozens of people wrote letters to the Fall River police, urging them to arrest Sullivan. Some people held the discriminatory belief that as an Irish immigrant, Sullivan was strong enough to wield a man's ax. They also believed that servants were not trustworthy. However, Lizzie's statement to the police placed Sullivan outside when Mrs. Borden was killed and upstairs in the attic bedroom during Mr. Borden's murder.

More Searches

The police were starting to believe that the murders must have been committed by someone inside the house. Lizzie and Sullivan were the only people known to have been there. However, police investigators were puzzled by the lack of blood found anywhere except on the victims. They also could not find a definite murder weapon.

On Friday, the day after the murders, the police returned to the Borden home to search it again. Whoever had hacked the Bordens to death must have gotten a good amount of blood on their clothing. Officers scoured the home looking for bloodstained clothing they could use as evidence. They found nothing. They asked Lizzie for the dress she was wearing that morning. She handed over a dark blue silk dress. It had no bloodstains on it.

AUTOPSY

After the family departed from the Bordens' gravesite, the police loaded the caskets of Andrew and Abby Borden back into the hearses. Their bodies were taken to the county medical examiner, Dr. William Dolan, to be autopsied. Dolan performed the autopsies in the lounge of the Oak Grove Cemetery on Thursday, August 11, 1892. Upon examining Mr. Borden's body, Dolan found ten wounds, concentrated on his head and face. The doctor found 18 head wounds when he examined Mrs. Borden's body.[3]

On Saturday after the funeral service, the police once again searched the Borden home. This time there were no family members present because they had gone to the cemetery. The police conducted a detailed search from cellar to attic. Officers pulled up pieces of carpet and removed wall trim. Again, they found no evidence.

Suspicion Falls on Lizzie Borden

As they investigated, the Fall River police became increasingly convinced that Lizzie was involved in the murders. She admitted to being at home at the time of the murders. She also had a motive because she stood to inherit a lot of money upon the deaths of her father and stepmother. After the murders, Lizzie took medication prescribed by Dr. Bowen, including morphine, to calm her nerves. When the police questioned her, Lizzie gave several confusing and inconsistent answers. She told them she was in the barn at the time of her father's murder. But when asked why, Lizzie gave different answers to different people. She told Bowen that she was out looking for some iron. To Alice Russell, she explained that she was looking for a piece of iron or tin to fix a screen. To the police, she gave a third explanation, saying that she was in the barn loft, eating pears and looking for lead to weigh down her fishing line.

In addition, Lizzie said her stepmother had gone out that morning after receiving a note from a sick friend. Yet no note

While people were hesitant at first to believe a woman like Lizzie could commit murder, she eventually became the main suspect.

A POSTPONED TRIP

Originally, Lizzie was not supposed to be home the day her father and stepmother were murdered. She had planned to be away that week with a group of friends at a holiday cottage in the seaside town of Marion, Massachusetts. However, Lizzie postponed her trip. When asked by the police about her changed plans, Lizzie explained that she decided to wait until Monday to leave because her presence was needed at a Sunday meeting for the Christian Endeavor Society. One of the members of the group of friends, Elizabeth Johnston, received a letter from Lizzie that allegedly explained the reason for her postponement. However, Johnston refused to discuss the letter with police. None of the other women who went to Marion would speak to the police about the Borden murders.

was ever found. No one came forward to claim writing such a note. Even the boy who supposedly delivered the note was never found. On the day of the murders, a police officer saw Dr. Bowen looking at scraps of paper. When asked about them, the doctor replied that the paper was a note about his daughter's upcoming visit. He threw the scraps onto the kitchen stove and burned them before the officer could clearly see them. Though the scraps of paper have raised some questions, no one has ever been able to verify what the papers were.

To verify Lizzie's story about being in the barn, one officer walked out to the barn loft to search for footprints. He found none on the dusty floor. The officer put his hand down in the hay to see if it left an impression in the loft. It did. As a result, he believed that no one had actually been in the loft that day or else there would have been some sort of prints left behind. Although suspicions were growing, the police still had no hard evidence linking Lizzie Borden to the crime.

CHAPTER FOUR

THE INQUEST

Convinced that Lizzie was involved in the murders, District Attorney Hosea Knowlton called for an inquest, a legal procedure used to gather information. The son of a minister, Knowlton had graduated from Harvard Law School and had his own successful private law practice before entering public service. He served as a state lawmaker before becoming the district attorney for the Southern District of Massachusetts. In this role, he was responsible for the investigation and prosecution of the Borden murders.

Gathering Information

In the courtroom on the second floor of the police station, Knowlton called for Sullivan to testify. Judge Josiah Blaisdell presided over the inquest. Although nervous, Sullivan answered Knowlton's questions to the best of her ability. Her story was straightforward and the same as what she had told the police

Lizzie, shown here in a courtroom sketch, was not under arrest when she appeared in court for an inquest.

WHAT IS AN INQUEST?

An inquest is a court proceeding held primarily to determine the cause of a person's death. It is often conducted by a judge and jury. Generally, an inquest is not held for deaths that occur due to natural causes such as old age or disease. Instead, an inquest is used to investigate sudden and unexpected deaths. At an inquest, people testify and answer questions, providing information for the police investigation. Suspects may be questioned, but because no accusation is officially presented, suspects are not allowed to defend themselves during an inquest. If they are later officially charged with a crime, they can present a defense during trial.

earlier. She had no additional information about where Lizzie had been on the morning of the murders.

Knowlton wanted to call Lizzie Borden to testify next, as she was the only other person in the house and was therefore a critical witness. She was also the main suspect. Andrew Jennings, the Borden family lawyer, asked to accompany Lizzie to the inquest, but his request was denied. Knowlton insisted that he was simply gathering information about the crime.

When Lizzie testified at the inquest, Knowlton questioned her about her father's financial situation. He wanted to establish whether money may have been a motive for murder, as Lizzie may have feared her father was leaving his estate to her stepmother instead of to his daughters. Lizzie answered that she had no knowledge of her father's will or whether he had made an agreement with her stepmother. She did say that she believed her uncle John Vinnicum Morse had mentioned something about her father having a will, but she couldn't remember when she heard this.

Knowlton also asked Lizzie whether she knew of any possible enemies her father or stepmother might have had. She mentioned that her father had a disagreement with a man over his refusal to rent property to him. But she could not recall the man's name. She also mentioned her uncle Hiram Harrington, who was married to Andrew Borden's sister, as not being friendly with her father. She could not name anyone who was on bad terms with her stepmother.

Next, Knowlton questioned Lizzie about her relationship with her stepmother. She admitted to having disagreements with her stepmother in the past, but she claimed that it was simply a difference of opinion. When asked whether the two women were on cordial terms, Lizzie said yes. "Quite cordial. I do not mean the dearest of friends in the world, but very kindly

WAS ANDREW BORDEN MAKING A WILL?

At the inquest, Lizzie testified she had no knowledge of her father having an existing will or planning to create one. Yet Andrew Borden may have been planning such a document. When John Vinnicum Morse testified at the inquest, he told Knowlton that at some point in the past year, Mr. Borden had spoken to him about making a will. Mr. Borden was interested in making some bequests to charitable causes. A bequest is a gift made through a will. Morse testified that he did not know if Mr. Borden had followed through on his intention to make a will.

feelings and pleasant. I do not know how to answer you any better than that," she said.[1] When Knowlton asked whether their relationship was like mother and daughter, Lizzie admitted that she no longer called Abby Borden "Mother," preferring instead to address her as "Mrs. Borden." Knowlton then asked whether Andrew and Abby Borden were happily married, and Lizzie said they were.

Knowlton asked about the clothes Lizzie was wearing on the morning of the murder. She testified that she had been wearing a navy blue silk skirt and a navy blue blouse in the morning. She had changed into a pink housedress in the afternoon.

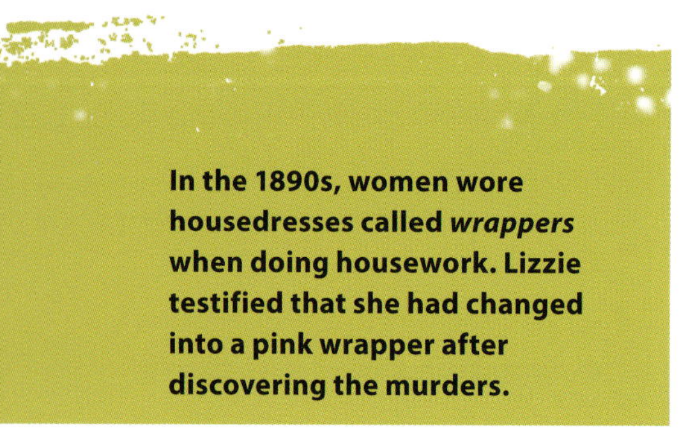

In the 1890s, women wore housedresses called *wrappers* when doing housework. Lizzie testified that she had changed into a pink wrapper after discovering the murders.

Confusing Answers

Throughout the questioning, Lizzie frequently gave confusing and contradictory answers. At first, she said she was in the kitchen looking at a magazine around the time her father arrived home. Then she said she might have been in the dining room. A few questions later, she said she might have been upstairs for a few minutes when her father came home. When Knowlton pointed out the difference in her answers, Lizzie appeared confused. "I don't know what I have said. I have answered so many questions and I am so confused I don't know one thing from another," she replied.[2]

When asked about her time in the barn, Lizzie said that she had gone to the barn shortly after her father returned home. She said she was searching for sinkers to use as weights on her fishing line. Knowlton heatedly questioned Lizzie about why she had spent so much time in the barn. Lizzie replied that she did not do things in a hurry. When asked if she did anything else in the barn loft, Lizzie said she ate a few pears while looking out the window. Knowlton was skeptical. "I ask you why you should select that place, which was the only place which would put you out of sight of the house, to eat those three pears in?" he asked. Lizzie replied, "I cannot tell you any reason."[3]

MORPHINE CONFUSION

After the Borden murders, Dr. Bowen initially gave Lizzie bromo caffeine, a remedy for headaches, to help calm her nerves. On August 5, he prescribed her a small amount of morphine for the same reason. Morphine is a highly addictive sedative and painkiller made from opium. In the days after the murder, he doubled Lizzie's dose, which she continued to take while she testified at the inquest. Later, at trial, Bowen testified that morphine in the quantities that Lizzie took could affect memory and cause hallucinations. Some people believed the morphine contributed to Lizzie's confusion at the inquest and partly explained why her answers to Knowlton's questions kept changing.

The Borden property included a main house and a barn. Lizzie testified that she was in the barn at the time of the murders.

Knowlton then turned his questioning back to the tension in the Borden household. He asked Lizzie about the trouble she had with her stepmother about five years earlier. While Lizzie had given short, terse answers to his questions up to this point, she thoroughly explained the trouble over the house that

Mr. Borden had bought for his wife's sister. Lizzie's testimony seemed to show how much the property disagreement still bothered her, years later.

Knowlton also asked Lizzie about her attempt to purchase prussic acid at a local drugstore. Lizzie said she was not the woman who tried to buy the prussic acid. However, three witnesses would later testify that they had seen Lizzie at the drugstore on the day in question.

Building a Case

The inquest testimonies of Emma Borden and Hiram Harrington confirmed that the property disagreement had caused significant tension between the daughters and their father and stepmother. Emma insisted, however, that it was she, and not Lizzie, who bore the real grudge against Abby Borden over it. Harrington testified that Lizzie spoke of her stepmother in an unfriendly way. Other witnesses such as Dr. Bowen and Adelaide Churchill confirmed the timeline and other details.

Knowlton called five more witnesses to testify, including Alice Russell. Russell remembered Lizzie telling her that she had gone to the barn to look for tin or lead to fix a window screen. She did not remember the detail of Lizzie's clothing that day. Russell did, however, provide insight into the Borden family relationships. She testified she did not think they were "congenial."[4]

Overall, the inquest painted a difficult picture. It showed the division between Mr. and Mrs. Borden and the Borden sisters. Beneath the surface, hostilities simmered. Additionally, it appeared almost impossible that a stranger could have snuck into the house on August 4 and committed the murders. Even if someone had managed to make their way into the house without being caught, it was highly unlikely that they could have remained hidden for the time necessary to kill both victims. Sullivan's account of her actions that morning was believable and was supported in part by Lizzie's testimony. Lizzie, however, had given vague and shifting explanations for her actions that morning. When she found her father's body, she made no attempt to find Mrs. Borden and tell her. Yet as people gathered at the house, Lizzie mentioned that maybe she had heard her stepmother return earlier. Her denial of her attempt to buy prussic acid was even more suspicious. If she had truly meant to use it to clean a sealskin cape, why had she not just said so at the inquest? For Knowlton and the police, all of it supported their belief that Lizzie was guilty. The inquest ended on Thursday, August 11, 1892. It resulted in a judge signing a warrant for Lizzie Borden's arrest.

A FALSE STORY

On October 10, 1892, the *Boston Globe* ran a sensational story that claimed Lizzie Borden was pregnant and had paid off Bridget Sullivan for her silence after the murders, among other incredible claims. However, it was quickly proven that the entire story was false. A young *Globe* reporter named Henry Trickey had paid a private detective for information, and the detective provided the fake story. In a rush to beat its rivals to the news, the *Globe* had not fact-checked the story before printing it. On October 12, the *Globe* retracted the entire story and printed a front-page apology to Lizzie Borden.

CHAPTER FIVE

THE ARREST

District Attorney Knowlton and Marshal Rufus Hilliard agreed that they should notify Lizzie's family lawyer, Andrew Jennings, about her impending arrest. With Jennings present, they arrested Lizzie. The arraignment, a court proceeding at which Lizzie would plead guilty or not guilty, was scheduled for the next day.

Charged with Murder

At the arraignment, the clerk of the court motioned for Lizzie to stand. He read the complaint charging her with homicide and asked for her plea. In a soft voice, Lizzie replied, "Not guilty." The clerk did not hear her response and asked her a second time. This time, Lizzie spoke loudly and clearly: "I am not guilty."[1]

For people charged with murder in 1892, there was no bail, which is the temporary release of a prisoner in exchange for the payment of bail money to guarantee they will show up at their

Lizzie's arraignment took place at the courthouse in Fall River.

Court House. Fall River, Mass.

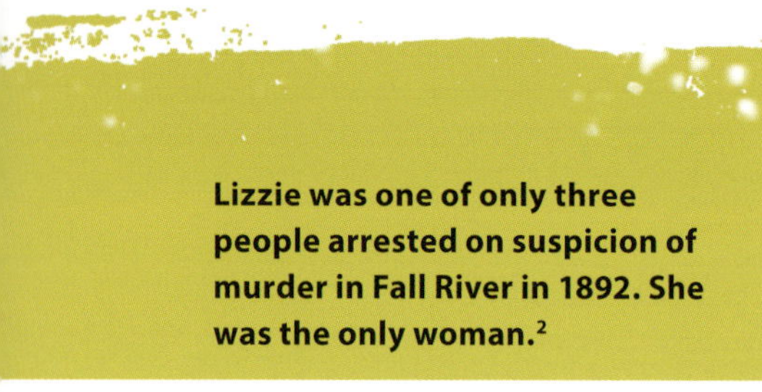

Lizzie was one of only three people arrested on suspicion of murder in Fall River in 1892. She was the only woman.[2]

court dates. Therefore, Lizzie would spend the next ten months in jail as she waited for her trial. Because Fall River did not have jail facilities for women, Lizzie was taken to the county jail in nearby Taunton, Massachusetts. When she arrived at the train station, it seemed as if the entire town had gathered to see her. The gruesome murders had thrust Lizzie into the public eye, and the case had become a topic of discussion for many people in the surrounding area.

Public Support

As Lizzie waited for trial, many people spoke out in her defense. The local chapter of the Christian Endeavor Society, based at Lizzie's church, adopted a resolution that expressed its sympathy for her and confidence that she would soon be

LIFE IN JAIL

At the Taunton jail, Lizzie discovered that the matron, Mary Jane Wright, was the mother of a childhood friend. While at the jail, Lizzie stayed in a small cell. It had a bed, a chair, and a washbowl. Even though it was jail, Lizzie was given several privileges. She was allowed to bring some books and a suitcase of clothing with her. The matron gave Lizzie one of her own soft pillows instead of the standard prison pillow. She was able to order dinner from the local hotel instead of eating the sparse prison meal. She received visits from her sister, her minister, and her lawyer.

Lizzie was jailed in the town of Taunton, which is about 15 miles (24 km) north of Fall River.

returned to her place with them. Chapters of the Women's Christian Temperance Union sent Lizzie telegrams of support. The organization also offered a public resolution of support for her that said, in part, "We would also declare our unshaken faith in [Lizzie Borden] as a fellow worker and sister tenderly beloved, and would assure her of our constant earnest prayers that she may be supported under the unprecedented trials and sorrows now resting upon her."[3] The Massachusetts Women's Christian Temperance Union circulated a petition demanding Lizzie be released on bail, despite the fact that bail was not legally an option for people charged with murder.

Others accused the police of unfairly persecuting Lizzie. They wrote letters to Marshal Hilliard and the press to express their displeasure. For example, Dr. S. P. Hubbard wrote, "I think the whole lot of you fellows better put your heads in soak. . . . The idea of trying to fasten the Butchery of Mr. Borden on his daughter and letting the fellow escape . . . is outrageous in the extreme."[4]

However, not everyone in Fall River was supportive of Lizzie. Some accused the police of treating her more favorably simply because of her social status. While many newspapers praised Lizzie for her calm manner, some questioned whether her cool demeanor during the investigation was a mask covering her true nature.

Preliminary Hearing

On Monday, August 22, 1892, Lizzie returned to Fall River for her preliminary hearing in court. Judge Josiah C. Blaisdell presided over the preliminary hearing. Lizzie's lawyer, Jennings, had objected to Judge Blaisdell, arguing that the judge had already presided over the inquest and would be prejudiced against his client. The judge ignored Jennings's argument.

To prove that Lizzie was "probably guilty" so that the case could be sent to a grand jury, District Attorney Knowlton only had to show that she was able to commit the murders and that she had a motive.[5] To do so, he called many witnesses to testify

Three hundred spectators and more than 30 reporters packed into the courthouse for Lizzie's preliminary hearing.[6]

WHAT IS A PRELIMINARY HEARING?

After a defendant has entered a plea of not guilty, a preliminary hearing is often held. The purpose of the preliminary hearing is to determine whether there is enough evidence to continue moving forward with the charges against the defendant. At the preliminary hearing, the prosecution will call witnesses and introduce evidence, while the defense can cross-examine witnesses. The defense cannot object to evidence presented by the prosecution at the preliminary hearing. However, evidence at the hearing is not always shown to the jury at trial. If the judge determines that there is probable cause to believe the defendant committed the crime, a trial will be scheduled. If not, the judge can dismiss the charges.

over several days. Each day, the courtroom was completely filled with lawyers, reporters, and members of the public who were engrossed by the gruesome details of the crime.

One of the key witnesses was Sullivan. After medical examiner Dr. William Dolan established that Abby Borden had been killed before her husband, Sullivan testified that she and Lizzie were the only two people in the house. Her testimony supported the prosecution's argument that Lizzie was the only person who had the opportunity to kill her stepmother and then her father that morning.

Another important witness was pharmacist Eli Bence. He testified that Lizzie had attempted to buy poison the day before the murders. Two other men who had been in the drugstore that day also testified that Lizzie had been there asking to buy the poison.

Lizzie's defense team argued that the prosecution had not found a murder weapon. No blood had been found linking her to the murders. They also noted that neighbors had reported hearing strange noises at night and seeing odd men around the neighborhood in the days leading up to the murders.

The preliminary hearing ended on September 1, 1892. As he gave his ruling, Judge Blaisdell asked the court to imagine how the situation would look if Lizzie were a man. He did not want them to let her go free simply because she was a woman, not someone they expected to be a murderer. He said:

> *Suppose for a single moment that a man was standing there. He was found close by that guest chamber which to Mrs. Borden was a chamber of death. Suppose that a man had been found in the vicinity of Mr. Borden and the only account he could give of himself was the unreasonable one that he was out in the barn looking for sinkers, that he was in the yard, that he was looking for something else. Would there be any question in the minds of men what should be done with such a man?*[7]

Several newspapers reported that Judge Josiah C. Blaisdell said Lizzie was "probably guilty," which may have unfairly influenced potential jurors before the trial.[8]

The judge ruled that there was enough evidence to move forward with the case against Lizzie Borden and ordered her to face a grand jury.

Grand Jury

On November 15, 1892, the grand jury took up the case. At first, jury members refused to issue an indictment, which is a formal criminal charge, in the case. However, they returned to hear new evidence from Lizzie's friend Alice Russell, who had stayed with the Borden sisters at the Borden house for a few days after the murders.

On December 1, Russell told the grand jury that she had seen Lizzie burn a dress. On August 7, three days after the murders, Russell had walked into the Bordens' kitchen and saw Lizzie standing at the stove with a skirt in her hand. Lizzie said she was going to burn the old skirt because it was covered in paint. Emma Borden was also in the kitchen at the time. Russell left the kitchen for a moment, and when she returned, Lizzie was ripping something that looked like the garment into pieces and burning them.

WHAT IS A GRAND JURY?

A grand jury listens to the prosecution's evidence in a case and decides whether there is enough evidence to send a case to trial. A grand jury is usually used in serious crimes. Unlike a preliminary hearing, a grand jury hearing is closed to the public. This allows witnesses to speak privately, without fear of retaliation from the public. It also protects the reputation of the accused person if the grand jury decides not to indict him or her for a crime.

The next day, Russell returned to the Borden home after being questioned by investigators about Lizzie's clothing the day of the murders. She said, "I am afraid, Lizzie, the worst thing you could have done was to burn that dress." Lizzie replied, "Oh, what made you let me do it? Why didn't you tell me?"[9] Although Emma would later testify at Lizzie's trial that it was her idea, not Lizzie's, to burn the dress because it was stained with

Lizzie burned a dress shortly after the murders. At the time, women wore dresses like this one, which is on display at a museum exhibit about Lizzie.

paint, Russell was no longer convinced of Lizzie's innocence. From this time forward, she believed Lizzie was probably guilty of the brutal crimes.

Russell's testimony, along with Sullivan's testimony that Lizzie had been wearing a blue dress on the morning of the murders, was enough for the grand jury. The jury decided to indict Lizzie for the murders of Andrew and Abby Borden. Lizzie was charged with first-degree murder due to the severity of the crime. If convicted on this charge, Lizzie would face the death penalty.

Insanity Plea

Unsure of whether he could win a case against a young woman in court, Knowlton came up with another idea. Perhaps he could convince Lizzie's attorneys to accept an insanity plea. If they did, the case would never go to trial. Knowlton consulted experts, but they declined to give an opinion on Lizzie's sanity. Knowlton and the police also interviewed people throughout Fall River to see if anyone believed the Borden family had a history of insanity. While many believed the Bordens were a little odd, no one thought them to be insane.

Knowlton then approached Lizzie's attorney and suggested that they order a psychological examination for Lizzie, perhaps to give her an insanity defense. Jennings refused. He believed that Lizzie would be proven innocent at trial.

CHAPTER SIX

THE PROSECUTION'S CASE

The trial of Lizzie Borden began on June 5, 1893, at the New Bedford Superior Court. Crowds gathered outside the courtroom. Around 11 o'clock in the morning, Lizzie arrived. Reporter Julian Ralph described her, saying, "She is, in truth, a very plain-looking old maid. She may be likened to a typical school marm, plain, practical and with a face that shows the deep lines of either care or habitual low spirits. . . . There is nothing wicked [or] criminal, or hard in her features."[1]

The prosecution was led by Knowlton and William H. Moody, the district attorney for Essex County, Massachusetts. Lizzie's defense team included Jennings and attorneys Melvin Adams and George D. Robinson, who was a former Massachusetts governor. On the first day, a jury of 12 men

Lizzie's trial took place at the courthouse in New Bedford, Massachusetts.

CHOOSING A JURY

On the first day of the Lizzie Borden trial, 150 prospective jurors were called in from the county voting registries and ordered to appear at the courthouse. Because of the intense interest in the trial in Fall River, the jurors were drawn from other areas of the county. One by one, the men were questioned by Judge Albert Mason. The prosecution and the defense were able to challenge certain jurors that they found to be unsuitable. After nine hours, a jury of 12 men—six farmers, three mechanics, two manufacturers, and one real estate owner—was chosen. The jurors were allowed to send telegrams to their families to inform them they would be serving the court. After swearing their oath, the jurors were taken to the Parker House hotel where they would live for the rest of the trial.[2]

was selected. The jurors were all men because at the time, women did not have the legal right to serve on juries. The next day, the prosecution opened its case against Lizzie.

The Prosecution Begins

Moody gave the prosecution's opening statement. He laid out the facts of the murders, described the Borden house and its location in town, and concluded that Lizzie must be responsible for the murders. He acknowledged that many people thought it was impossible for a woman like Lizzie to have committed such a violent crime. Yet he described Lizzie as the only person to have both motive and opportunity. He pulled out a small hatchet that was broken at the base of its wooden handle and identified it as the possible murder weapon. Then he reached for a black bag to reveal the wounded skulls of Andrew and Abby Borden. According to newspaper reports, Lizzie fainted at the sight of the skulls. After Lizzie was revived by smelling salts and given a few minutes to compose herself, the trial continued.

In his opening statement, Moody outlined the prosecution team's three-part case against Lizzie. First, they wanted to prove that Lizzie had motive and the state of mind to commit the crime. Second, they wanted to show that she had the opportunity and means to commit the murders. Third, they aimed to prove that Lizzie's pattern of lies and contradictions showed she knew she was guilty.

Witnesses for the Prosecution

With the opening statement concluded, the prosecution began calling its list of witnesses to testify before the court. The first

ANOTHER MURDER

On May 30, 1893, 22-year-old Bertha Manchester was killed in her Fall River home. Like the Bordens, Bertha was killed with an ax or hatchet in the middle of the day. It was only a few days before the scheduled start of Lizzie's trial, and some people wondered whether the murders were connected. As Lizzie was in custody at the time of Manchester's murder, it was impossible for her to have committed this crime. The day before Lizzie's trial began, the police arrested an immigrant farm laborer in connection with the murder of Manchester. The arrest seemed to indicate that the Manchester and Borden murders were not connected, because the laborer was not in the United States when the Bordens were killed. By the time the press reported the laborer's arrest, the jurors in the Lizzie Borden case had already been ordered not to read the newspaper. It is likely that the jurors did not know that the murder of Manchester was not connected to the Bordens' murders.

LOCATIONS IN THE LIZZIE BORDEN CASE

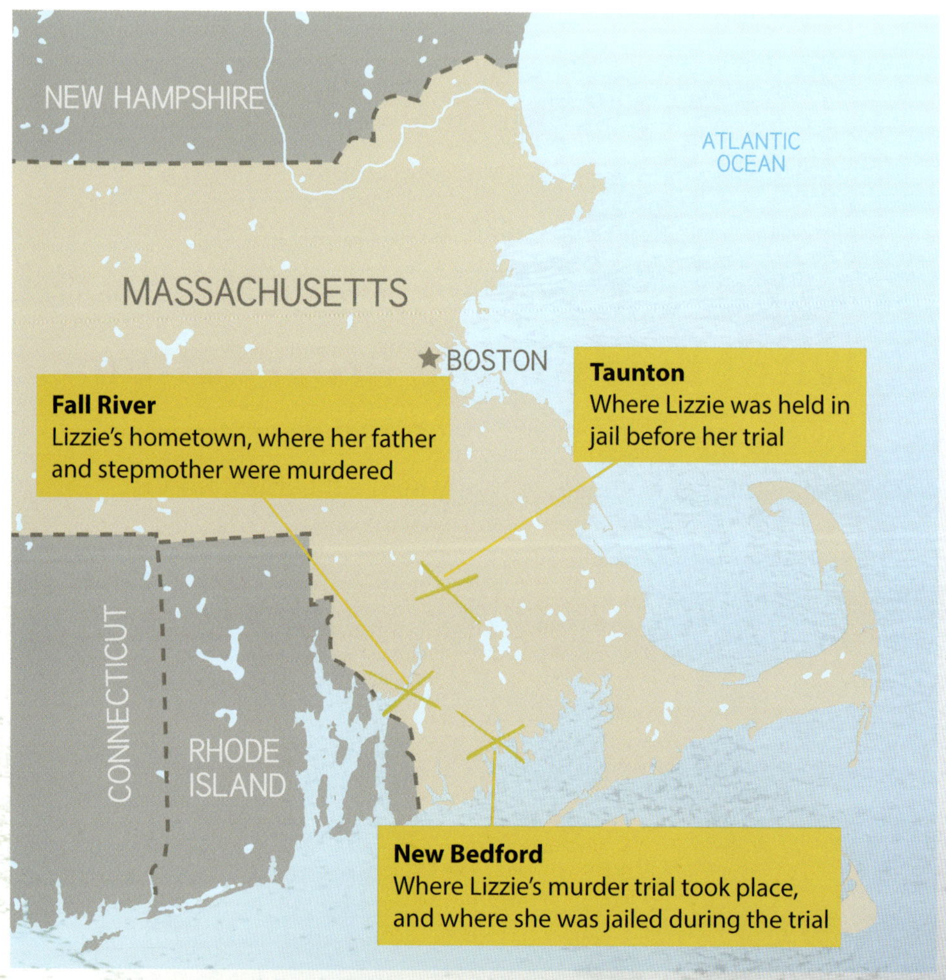

witnesses testified about events in and around the Borden home on August 4, 1892. After each witness testified, the defense was allowed to cross-examine or question them about their testimony. The jurors were also taken to Fall River for a tour of the Borden house and property and the surrounding neighborhood.

One of the witnesses, Thomas Kieran, was a civil engineer who had prepared diagrams of the Borden house for the prosecution's case. When testifying about his diagrams, Kieran explained that he had also decided to perform several line-of-sight experiments at the Borden home to try to figure out how the murderer and the victims' bodies could have remained out of sight for so long. When questioned about these by the defense, Kieran said that a person could have easily stood inside the front hall closet without being seen. In addition, he testified that he had his assistant lie on the guest room floor in the same way that Mrs. Borden's body was found. When Kieran went up and down the stairs, there was only one spot where he could see his assistant. Even then, he said it was because he was looking for him. At all other parts of the stairs, Kieran could not see his assistant lying on the floor in the guest room.

The prosecution also called Sullivan as a witness. She testified that Lizzie was the only person she saw in the Borden home at the time of the murders. However, she could not confirm that there was a poor relationship between Lizzie and her stepmother. She insisted that she had not seen conflict or quarrelling during her time working for the family. Under intense questioning from the defense, Sullivan admitted that it might have been possible for her to have left the screen door on the side of the house unlocked. That meant it was possible that an intruder may have come inside without being detected. Sullivan also testified that Lizzie had been wearing a blue dress with darker blue figures on it that morning.

HANNAH GIFFORD'S TESTIMONY

One of the prosecution's witnesses, dressmaker Hannah Gifford, testified to a conversation she had had with Lizzie about Abby Borden. The conversation showed Lizzie's animosity toward her stepmother. Gifford had worked for the Bordens as a seamstress. About five months before the murders, Gifford referred to Mrs. Borden as Lizzie's mother. Lizzie immediately snapped at her and called Mrs. Borden "a mean good-for-nothing." Gifford protested. "Oh Lizzie, you don't mean that?" she said. Lizzie replied, "Yes, I don't have much to do with her; I stay in my room most of the time."[3]

The next group of witnesses had been at the Borden house shortly after the discovery of the murders. Dr. Seabury Bowen testified that Lizzie had told him she had been in the barn looking for lead sinkers at the time of her father's murder. He also testified that he had prescribed morphine to Lizzie after the murders, which may have affected her inquest testimony. Adelaide Churchill, the Bordens' neighbor, testified that Lizzie had been wearing a light blue dress with darker blue diamond figures on it. She did not see any blood on the dress. The witnesses agreed that Lizzie had changed her dress after the bodies had been discovered. She had been wearing a pink wrapper when interviewed by the police.

Alice Russell told the court about Lizzie's visit with her the night before the murders, when Lizzie had told her she felt as if something was hanging over her and that she feared the family's milk could be poisoned. She also recounted the time she had seen Lizzie burning a blue dress days after the murders. During cross-examination, defense lawyer George Robinson highlighted the point that the police were at the house when Russell saw Lizzie burning the dress. He argued that if burning

WHAT DRESS WAS LIZZIE WEARING?

When the police asked Lizzie to turn over the dress she had been wearing the morning of the murders, she gave them a fancy, dark blue dress. The dress was spotless, with no bloodstains. Several witnesses could not confirm that they had seen Lizzie wearing that dress on the day of the murders. Some testified that she wore a light blue dress with dark figures. Others said it was a calico fabric. Some could not remember at all. Only Mrs. Bowen, the doctor's wife, identified the dark blue dress that Lizzie had given to the prosecution as the one she had worn that morning. To confuse the issue, Russell testified that she had seen Lizzie burning a light blue dress a few days after the murders. That dress was ruined with brown paint.

the dress had something to do with the murders, Lizzie would have hidden it from the police.

Assistant Marshal Fleet was another key witness. He testified that Lizzie had corrected him when he called Abby Borden her mother. When looking for a murder weapon at the Borden home, police had found two axes and two hatchets on the cellar floor. Moody produced these weapons, and Fleet

Police found axes and hatchets similar to these at the Borden home after the murders, but none were proven to be the murder weapon.

confirmed for the court that they were the weapons found in the Borden home. Fleet said that when he went to search Lizzie's room on the day of the murders, Lizzie reluctantly agreed but asked him to search as quickly as possible. Finding nothing in the room, Fleet returned to the cellar, where he found a box containing a hatchet with its handle broken off. The break in the wood handle was new and close to the head. The other items in the box were covered with dust, but the handleless hatchet was covered in ash on both sides.

Fleet also testified that he had searched the home again after the Bordens' funeral services on Saturday. He looked through an upstairs clothes closet. He did not find a dress with bloodstains or paint stains. If Lizzie had burned a paint-stained dress the next day, where was it when Fleet searched the house?

Inquest Testimony Tossed

The prosecution wanted to introduce Lizzie's inquest testimony, full of contradictions and puzzling statements, as evidence at the trial. However, the defense objected and claimed that Lizzie had not testified voluntarily at the inquest. They argued that although she had not yet been charged with murder at the time of the inquest, she was treated as if she had been charged. As such, the lawyers argued, Lizzie had been denied her rights to due process under the law. She was not allowed to have her

ELI BENCE'S TESTIMONY

Pharmacist Eli Bence's testimony sparked another objection from the defense. Bence testified that prussic acid was not used to clean sealskin or any other type of cape. The defense argued that Lizzie's alleged attempt to buy poison was not relevant to the murders for which she was on trial. The prosecution argued that the testimony showed her state of mind just prior to the murders, which was relevant. The judges spoke and then announced that the prosecution needed to find witnesses to back up Bence's opinion that prussic acid could not be used for sealskin. The next morning, the prosecution presented a pharmacist, a chemist, and a furrier as witnesses. However, when the defense asked the chemist if prussic acid could be used to kill moths in sealskin, the chemist said that it could. The judges ruled that Bence's testimony would be excluded from the trial.

lawyer present during the inquest and was never warned about her right to remain silent under the Fifth Amendment of the US Constitution. Additionally, she had been under the influence of prescribed morphine at the time of her inquest testimony.

Knowlton argued that the inquest had followed the law and that Lizzie's testimony should be used as evidence in the trial. However, the three-judge panel sided with the defense and ruled that Lizzie had been essentially under arrest at the inquest. Therefore, her inquest testimony was not presented as evidence to the jury at the trial.

Closing Arguments

Knowlton delivered the prosecution's closing arguments. While he acknowledged that it was hard to imagine that a woman could be guilty of such a horrific crime, he reminded the jurors that women were human just like men. "They are no better than we; they are no worse than we," he said.[4]

Knowing that the jurors would find it difficult to believe that Lizzie had killed her own father in cold blood, Knowlton suggested that she had planned her stepmother's murder, but not her father's. "It was . . . malice against Mrs. Borden that inspired the assassin. It was Mrs. Borden whose life that wicked person sought; and all the motive that we have to consider . . . bears on her," he said.[5] Knowlton argued that Lizzie had killed her father without planning once she realized that he would know who had killed her stepmother. Once Mr. and Mrs. Borden were dead, Knowlton asserted, Lizzie had tried to cover up the crime.

Knowlton dismissed the idea that a stranger had entered the house and killed the Bordens. He argued that evidence in the case pointed to Lizzie committing the murders. As he finished his statement, Knowlton said, "I submit these facts to you with the confidence that you are men of courage and truth."[6]

CHAPTER SEVEN

LIZZIE BORDEN'S DEFENSE

Once the prosecution finished presenting its case against Lizzie, it was the defense's turn. On June 15, 1893, Andrew Jennings, the Borden family's lawyer, gave an opening statement. He spoke for about forty minutes, emphasizing Lizzie's impeccable reputation, her good works in the community, and her general demeanor. "We shall show you that this young woman . . . had apparently led an honorable, spotless life; she was a member of the church; she was interested in church matters; she was connected with various organizations for charitable work; she was ever ready to help in any good thing, in any good deed," he said.[1]

Jennings reminded the jury that Lizzie, like all defendants accused of a crime, was presumed innocent. He reminded

Defense lawyers argued that as a woman in high society, Lizzie could not have committed murder.

PRESUMPTION OF INNOCENCE

One of the basic principles of a criminal trial in the United States is that a defendant is presumed innocent until proven guilty. Under this principle, the defense does not have to prove that a defendant is innocent. Instead, the prosecution must prove in its case that the defendant is guilty, beyond a reasonable doubt. If there is any reasonable doubt that the defendant committed the crime, then jurors are obligated to vote to acquit, which means to declare someone not guilty. The presumption of innocence is an important part of a fair trial, which is a right guaranteed by the Sixth Amendment of the US Constitution.

them that if there was any reasonable doubt regarding her guilt, she must be found not guilty. Jennings then spoke of the flawed legal case against Lizzie. He called the prosecution's case "wholly and absolutely circumstantial" and warned of the dangers of circumstantial evidence.[2] Circumstantial evidence is evidence that implies a person committed a crime but does not directly prove they did it. He told the jurors that it was not their job to solve the mystery of the Bordens' murders. He said they must only determine whether the prosecution supplied the proof required by law to show that Lizzie had committed the murders and that there was no opportunity for anyone else to have done so.

Jennings listed the holes in the prosecution's case and summed up his opening argument, saying, "There is no blood, not a spot on her hands, her head, her dress, or any part of her, no connection with any weapon whatever shown by any direct evidence in this case: with an opportunity for others to do the deed; with herself in the barn as it was done."[3] As Jennings spoke, Lizzie wiped tears from her eyes.

Poking Holes in the Prosecution's Case

The defense's strategy was simple. They did not need to answer the question of who had killed the Bordens. They simply had to show that the prosecution's case was not strong enough to prove that Lizzie had done it. To this end, the defense spent a considerable amount of time discrediting the prosecution's witnesses and pointing out the inconsistencies in their testimonies. For example, in his cross-examination of Sullivan when she testified for the prosecution, Robinson was able to get Sullivan to confirm her earlier testimony from the inquest that the Bordens and Lizzie did sometimes eat meals together in the dining room. He also got her to admit that it was possible she left the screen

MELVIN O. ADAMS

Lizzie's attorney, Jennings, knew that he would need help for the murder trial. One of the lawyers he hired to join the defense team was Melvin O. Adams, a Boston lawyer who had previously been an assistant district attorney. Adams had a strong record both as a prosecutor and as a defense lawyer. During Lizzie's trial, he was responsible for cross-examining the prosecution's key witnesses, especially those who were scientific or medical experts.

door unlocked and that a person could have entered the house without her seeing him.

When questioned by the defense, Dr. Bowen explained that he had prescribed morphine to Lizzie, which may have affected her testimony at the inquest. The defense also discredited the prosecution's theory that the dress Lizzie had worn while committing the murders was the same one she burned in front of Russell. Under defense questioning, Russell admitted that while she could identify which dress Lizzie burned, she did not remember what Lizzie was wearing the morning of the murders.

The defense also cast doubt on witnesses' ability to remember Lizzie's dress. Adelaide Churchill testified that Sullivan was wearing a light-colored calico dress that day, but Sullivan herself said she was wearing a dark, indigo blue dress. If Churchill was wrong about Sullivan's dress, then how could the jury rely on her testimony that Lizzie had been wearing a light blue patterned dress that morning? A third witness, Bowen's wife, added further confusion to the matter of the dress. She testified that Lizzie wore the dark blue silk dress that Lizzie had handed over to the police.

Police Errors

The defense also sought to show that the police had made several errors in the investigation of the Borden murders. The prosecution argued that the handleless hatchet was probably the murder weapon and that the murderer had destroyed the hatchet's handle to hide evidence. Fleet had testified that he had found the hatchet head in a box with no handle nearby. However, Officer Michael Mullaly contradicted Fleet's testimony. He said that there was a broken-off handle in the box and that Fleet had removed it.

The defense's questioning revealed other police errors. Fleet admitted that Lizzie's closet was not searched at first. Another officer admitted that he had lost the list of clothing in Lizzie's closet. As a result, no one knew if there was a light blue dress in the house at the time of the police search.

During the trial, Lizzie lived in the jail across the street from the New Bedford courthouse instead of traveling back and forth to her jail cell in Taunton.

While questioning the prosecution's medical experts, the defense noted there had been no trace of poison in either victim's body. This raised doubt about the theory that their sickness the day before was due to an unsuccessful poisoning. When the defense asked a medical expert about how hard it would be to remove blood from a hatchet, the doctor noted several places on a hatchet head where it would have been almost impossible to remove all traces of blood. In addition, the doctor noted that there was dirt still on the hatchet head. Together, this testimony contradicted the prosecution's theory that the hatchet head was the murder weapon and had been freshly washed to remove all blood.

Odd Noises and Strange People

Next the defense called a series of witnesses who testified that there had been odd noises and strange people around the Bordens' neighborhood shortly before the murders. Neighbor Marthe Chagnon testified that she had heard a strange noise at around eleven o'clock the night before the murders. Charles

A museum exhibit shows a photo of Andrew Borden's body at the crime scene.

Gifford and Uriah Kirby testified that they had seen a strange man near the Borden house the night before the murders around the same time. Another witness described a man with a brown hat and a black coat sitting in an open buggy in front of the Borden house around eleven o'clock on the morning of the murders. Benjamin Handy testified that he had seen a medium-sized young man with a pale complexion who was acting strangely near the Borden home the day of the murders.

Another group of witnesses testified about how easy it was to get into the house after the murders. The day after the murders, Jerome Borden, a cousin of Andrew Borden, walked right in the front door, suggesting that the spring lock on the door was not secure. Walter Stevens, a reporter for the *Fall River Daily Evening News*, had also entered the house. He was able to walk around the house and yard. In the barn, he saw at least three other people going up the barn stairs, which contradicted Fleet's account that the barn was undisturbed before he investigated it and cast doubt on police statements that Lizzie's alibi of being in the barn loft was suspect because the dust in the loft appeared to be undisturbed.

Emma Borden Takes the Stand

Emma Borden was the defense's primary witness. Jennings questioned Emma about her sister's financial situation to show that money was not a motive for murder. Emma produced records that showed her sister had nearly $3,000 in the bank and numerous shares of stock. In 1892, this was a substantial amount of money for a single woman.

Next, Jennings asked Emma to testify about the relationship between her sister and her father. She noted that they were close and told the court about the gold ring that her sister had given to her father, which he wore until his death. On the subject of Lizzie's dress, Emma testified that she was the one who had urged Lizzie to burn the dress because it was ruined from paint stains and badly faded. When questioned by Knowlton, Emma insisted that Lizzie and Mrs. Borden were cordial. She portrayed herself as having the more strained relationship with her stepmother.

A FIGHT BETWEEN SISTERS?

During the preliminary hearing in August 1893, Lizzie was housed in the jail apartment at the Fall River Police Station and was supervised by the jail's matron for female prisoners, Hanna Reagan. Matron Reagan testified during Lizzie's trial that she overheard an argument in loud voices between Lizzie and Emma Borden while Lizzie was staying there. Lizzie declared, "You gave me away, Emma, didn't you?" Emma replied to her sister, "I only told Mr. Jennings what I thought he ought to know." Lizzie responded, "Remember, Emma, that I will never give in one inch, never."[4] Lying on the bed, Lizzie turned away from Emma and refused to speak to her any more. In her trial testimony, Emma strongly denied that any such argument had occurred.

Lizzie, *center-left*, sits in court with her sister, Emma, who is covering her face with her hand.

Closing Arguments

After the defense had called all of its witnesses, Robinson delivered the defense team's closing argument. Dressed in a plain black suit, he spoke for almost four hours. He acknowledged the horror of the crimes. He insisted that the killer must be a maniac, not someone as respectable as Lizzie Borden. He dismissed the prosecution's case as circumstantial and asserted that it had failed to prove that Lizzie was guilty beyond a reasonable doubt. Robinson said, "Now there is absolutely no direct evidence against Miss Borden, the defendant. . . . Nobody saw or heard anything or experienced anything that connects her with the tragedies. No weapon whatever, and no knowledge of the use of one, as to her, has been shown."[5] He pointed out that no blood had been found

LIZZIE'S STATE OF MIND

In a letter to her friend, Mrs. William Lindsey Jr., on May 11, 1893, a few weeks before the beginning of her trial, Lizzie Borden showed that the stress of her situation was weighing on her heavily. She wrote:

> *My spirits are at ebb tide. I can see no ray of light amid the gloom. I try to fill up the waiting time as well as I can, but every day is longer and longer. I begin to think the tangled threads will never be smoothed out. My friend—do not make any plans for me at Christmas. I do not expect to be free. . . . You know my life can never be the same again if I ever come home. Forgive me for this sober letter, but my heart is heavy and the burden laid upon me seems greater than I can bear.*[6]

on Lizzie or any piece of her clothing, something that would have been impossible if she had been the killer. He argued that the murders may have easily been committed by an intruder who slipped in and out of the house without being seen.

Robinson presented Lizzie to the jurors as a woman similar to their own wives and daughters. He reasoned a key defense argument—that a woman like Lizzie could not have committed these brutal murders. He reminded the jurors of the viciousness of the attacks, how the murderer must have stood over Abby Borden and leaned over Andrew Borden's head to deliver the fatal blows. "Such acts as those are morally and physically impossible for this young woman defendant," he said.[7] Robinson highlighted the inconsistency between the assumed maniac who murdered two people and the young woman in the courtroom. "Gentlemen, as you look upon her you will pass your judgment that she is not insane. To find her guilty you must believe she is a fiend. Does she look it? . . . Have you seen anything that shows the lack of human feeling and womanly bearing?" he said.[8] Then Robinson thanked the jurors and urged them to return a verdict of not guilty.

CHAPTER EIGHT

THE VERDICT

On June 20, 1893, the final day of the trial, the judge asked Lizzie if she wanted to say anything to the jury. On her lawyers' advice, she had not taken the stand during the trial to defend herself. Now, she stood and said in a clear voice, "I am innocent. I leave it to my counsel to speak for me."[1]

The Jury Deliberates

Judge Justin Dewey, one of the three judges in the case, addressed the jury. As a judge, Dewey was supposed to give the jurors the legal instructions they needed to weigh the evidence and come to a decision on Lizzie's guilt or innocence. However, he clearly sympathized with Lizzie and reminded the jurors of her good character and charitable work. He also reminded jurors that the fact that Lizzie did not testify at her own trial was not an indication of her guilt.

Judge Dewey spoke about some of the prosecution's claims. In regard to the note that arrived for Mrs. Borden that morning

Lizzie, *left*, in court during her trial

The jury in the trial of Lizzie Borden was composed of white men. At the time, women did not have the legal right to serve on juries, and people of color were generally excluded from juries due to discrimination.

from a sick friend, Judge Dewey asked about what motive Lizzie would have to lie about the note when it would have been much simpler to just say that her stepmother had left the house. Instead, he suggested that the real killer may have sent the note and then destroyed the evidence after the murders.

Judge Dewey urged the jurors to consider the testimony of the prosecution's medical experts carefully. He said, "It is a matter of frequent observation to see experts of good standing expressing conflicting and irreconcilable views upon questions arising at a trial. They sometimes manifest a bias or partisan spirit in favor of the party employing them."[2] Judge Dewey also warned the jurors not to consider any information from outside the trial as they deliberated the case. He urged them to consider the evidence impartially and thoughtfully and to seek the truth. It was rare for a judge to give instructions that so strongly supported the innocence of the defendant.

After receiving the judge's instructions, the 12 jurors walked into the jury room where they would consider the evidence and determine their verdict. The wait would not be long. Less than an hour and half later, the jurors signaled that they had come to a verdict.

A Unanimous Verdict

The courtroom filled again to hear the jury's verdict. The court clerk asked Lizzie to stand. Then he asked, "Gentlemen of the jury, have you agreed upon your verdict?" The head juror replied, "We have." As the clerk asked for the verdict, the juror interrupted the question and declared, "Not guilty."[3]

The spectators in the courtroom erupted into applause. Lizzie dropped into her seat, placed her face on the rail in front of her, and cried. The clerk continued: "Gentlemen of the jury, you, upon your oaths, do say that Lizzie Andrew Borden, the prisoner at the bar, is not guilty?"[4] All of the jurors confirmed that their verdict was unanimous. Lizzie Borden was found not guilty.

JURY DELIBERATIONS

Different accounts of what happened in the jury room emerged after the verdict. One said the jurors argued over their decision and almost broke out into a fight. Another rumor said that one juror promised free liquor to the other jurors if they voted for an acquittal. However, the truth was much less interesting. When they first entered the jury room, the jurors took an informal vote. It was unanimous to acquit. They spent a little time discussing some of the evidence before taking an official vote. They all voted for acquittal. Then they stayed in the jury room for an additional 30 minutes, out of respect for the prosecution, as jury members did not want to appear as if they didn't consider the prosecution's work and evidence.

After the verdict was read, many in the courtroom celebrated. They waved their handkerchiefs and rushed to congratulate Lizzie. Knowlton and Moody congratulated the defense team. Jennings helped Lizzie to her feet and put his arm around her. Lizzie hugged her sister Emma and said, "I want to go home; take me straight home tonight. . . . I want to see the old place and settle down at once."[5]

After leaving the courtroom, Lizzie began the hour-long journey to Fall River by carriage. Thousands of people gathered on the streets of the town, celebrating the verdict and waiting to welcome Lizzie home. However, instead of going to the Borden home on Second Street, Lizzie spent a quieter night at the home of friends. There, she answered letters and telegrams from well-wishers near and far.

Newspapers praised the verdict. An editorial in the *New York Times* on June 21, 1893, explained, "It will be a certain

LIZZIE'S COURT PROCEEDINGS

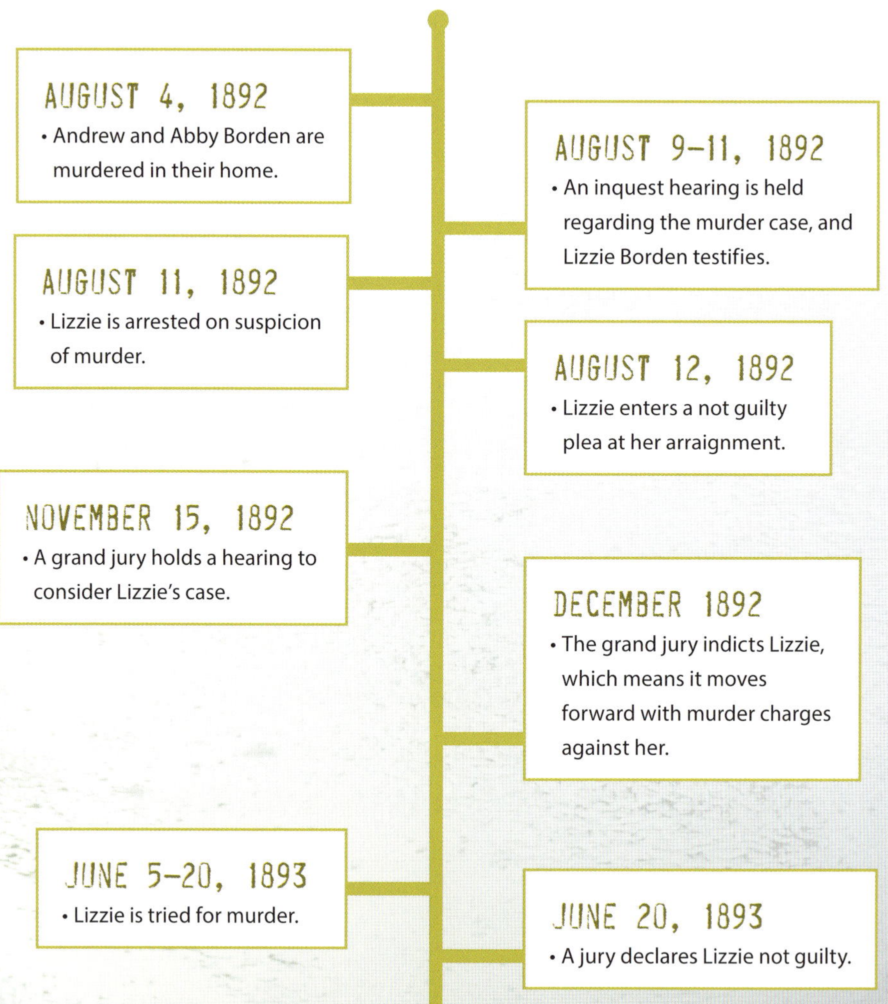

relief to every right-minded man or woman who has followed the case to learn that the jury at New Bedford has not only acquitted Miss Lizzie Borden of the atrocious crime with which she was charged, but has done so with a promptness that was very significant."[6] The *Times* blamed the police for the charges against Lizzie, stating:

> *The police are of the usual inept and stupid and muddle-headed sort that such towns manage to get for themselves. There is nothing more merciless than the vanity of ignorant and untrained men charged with the detection of crime, in the face of a mystery that they cannot solve, and for the solution of which they feel themselves responsible.*[7]

New Doubts Emerge

Many people wondered what Lizzie would do, now that she had been acquitted. Some believed that she and her sister Emma would move to New York City or to Europe, where they could change their names and live without the celebrity caused by the sensational trial. However, Lizzie decided to remain in Fall River.

It was not long before public opinion began to turn against Lizzie. While many people had supported her during the trial, now they began to have new doubts. If Lizzie hadn't killed her stepmother and father, who had? Many of the town's working-class people had never believed in her innocence. They felt that Lizzie was protected because of her social status in town. Her previous supporters, many of the town's upper-class residents, increasingly began to avoid her. Her circle of friends and acquaintances shrank. The Central Congregational Church, where she had spent a lot of time doing charity work, no longer welcomed her. When she attended a Sunday service in July 1893, no one sat in the pews around her. As the years passed, more and more people believed that Lizzie had gotten away with murder. The Fall River police never reopened the Borden case to look for another suspect, adding to the public's increasing belief in Lizzie's guilt.

A New Life

Not long after Lizzie's return to Fall River, she and Emma moved out of the Second Street house. With their sizable inheritance from their father's estate, the sisters purchased a larger, more

THE FALL RIVER TRAGEDY

Less than two months after the verdict, Edwin Porter, a reporter for the *Fall River Daily Globe* newspaper, published the first book about the Borden murders, *The Fall River Tragedy: A History of the Borden Murders*. The book was mainly a collection of Porter's articles for the *Globe* and contained numerous false statements about the Borden family and the murders, with little new information. When Lizzie learned about Porter's planned book, she was upset. Her lawyer, Jennings, contacted Porter and warned him that he would be held accountable for any false statements in the book. In addition, Jennings met with Porter and came to an agreement that no photographs of living Borden family members would be included in the book.

A FOUND HATCHET

In June 1893, a young boy climbed up to the roof of a barn behind the Borden property. He had been playing baseball with friends and went to retrieve a lost baseball. On the roof, the boy found a weather-beaten hatchet with a 3.5-inch (8.9 cm) blade. It was the same size as the blade thought to have killed the Bordens. The found hatchet still had a slight coloring of gilt, showing that it was very new when lost. Similar gilt metal had been found in one of Mrs. Borden's wounds. Some people believed that the murderer had thrown the hatchet onto the roof as he escaped out the back of the house. Others were more skeptical. They believed someone put the hatchet there to be found by the boys and create a stir.

expensive home on the Hill, the city's elite residential area. The new home was surrounded by maple trees and had more modern features than the Second Street house. Lizzie named the new house "Maplecroft" and had the name chiseled into its granite steps.

Lizzie also started going by the name "Lizbeth." She regularly attended theater shows in Boston and stopped most of her charitable work. She developed a close friendship with an actress named Nance O'Neil. After one of O'Neil's shows, Lizzie invited the entire cast to a lavish party at Maplecroft, complete with a full orchestra and champagne.

Lizzie's new friends and lifestyle drove a wedge between her and her sister. In 1905, Emma moved out of Maplecroft and never spoke to Lizzie again. Many of their mutual friends also stopped speaking to Lizzie.

After being found not guilty, Lizzie and Emma purchased a new 14-room home in Fall River. Lizzie called the house Maplecroft, and she lived there for the rest of her life.

A Social Outcast

Even though she had become a social outcast in Fall River, Lizzie remained at Maplecroft for the rest of her life. She loved animals, especially her pet Boston terriers. She employed several staff and treated them well. She befriended the children of her staff members and treated them with ice cream and birthday wishes. She quietly took part in some charitable work, donating books and caring for animals. She never publicly commented about the murder case.

In Fall River, giving a house a name, as Lizzie did with Maplecroft, was unusual and considered by some people to be offensive.

Lizzie Borden died quietly at Maplecroft on June 1, 1927, at age 67. She was buried near her father in the Borden family plot at Fall River's Oak Grove Cemetery. Her sister Emma died ten days later and was buried next to her sister.

TAUNTS AND PRANKS

The life of the Borden sisters at Maplecroft was not without its challenges. In May 1899, the police were summoned to the house. Lizzie reported that local boys and girls were throwing gravel and sand at her windows, and she wanted the police to make it stop. In 1902, Maplecroft again became the target of local youth. Over several nights, local youth trampled the lawn, threw rotten eggs at the side of the house, rang the doorbell at all hours of the night, and called Lizzie vile names when she answered the door.

CHAPTER NINE

WHO KILLED THE BORDENS?

More than a century after the murders of Andrew and Abby Borden, the public is still fascinated by the Borden case. After Lizzie's acquittal, no one else was ever charged with the murders. So, was Lizzie guilty, and the prosecution was simply unable to prove it? Or was there another killer who managed to avoid the police? Three years before Lizzie's death, true crime author Edmund Lester Pearson wrote, "The Borden case is without parallel in the criminal history of America. It is the most interesting and perhaps the most puzzling murder which has occurred in this country."[1]

Many researchers and crime experts have studied the Lizzie Borden trial transcripts and have pored over the evidence of the case. Most have concluded that Lizzie was guilty. Yet some suggest that another person may have been the murderer. Some point to the housemaid, Bridget Sullivan, while others

More than 100 years later, people remain interested in Lizzie Borden. She is featured by museums and in pop culture.

the True Story of
LIZZIE BORDEN
The Magic Parlor
BOOKS

suspect family members John Vinnicum Morse or Emma Borden. Still others believe that an unidentified killer snuck in and out of the Borden home without being seen. Without proof, no one can say for sure who the killer was.

The Investigation Today

Perhaps the outcome would have been different if the Borden murders had occurred today. The investigation would have been handled much differently. First, the crime scene would have been secured immediately by police, meaning people would not have been able to freely walk in and out as they did with the Borden house in the days after the murders. Doctors, neighbors, and reporters were allowed to come and go from the Borden house, and Lizzie and Sullivan were allowed to stay there as police investigated. Police questioned Lizzie and other residents inside the house. Because Lizzie and Sullivan were allowed

ANDREW JENNINGS'S JOURNALS

Andrew Jennings kept two handwritten journals during Lizzie's trial. Jennings's grandson, who died in 2011, left the journals to the Fall River Historical Society. Jennings's grandson had previously kept the journals private because he was concerned that researchers might misquote Jennings because his handwriting is difficult to read. Historians have hoped that the journals could provide fresh insights into the 1892 murders and trial.

to stay in the house, which was also the crime scene, they would have had plenty of time to hide and destroy evidence.

Today, yellow crime scene tape would immediately be put up around the outside of the house and property. No one beyond official investigators would be allowed inside. A crime

The way police investigate crime scenes today is much more strict than the procedures followed in the 1800s, when the Bordens were murdered.

LIZZIE BORDEN'S ESTATE

When Lizzie died in 1927, she left an estate valued at nearly $311,000. Of that amount, approximately $175,000 was personal property and $136,000 was real estate. Her home, Maplecroft, was not part of her estate. Because Lizzie had purchased the property with her sister, the property legally became Emma's upon Lizzie's death. In her will, Lizzie left nothing to her sister and stated that Emma already had her share of their father's estate, which was enough to make her comfortable. She left $30,000 and some shares of stock to the Animal Rescue League of Fall River and another $2,000 to its Washington, DC, chapter. Lizzie left the rest of her estate to personal friends, advisers, and employees.[2]

scene unit, state police, medical examiner, and district attorney would be notified and probably called to the scene. Any persons of interest or potential witnesses would have been removed from the house and taken to the police station for questioning. The Bordens would not have been allowed back into the house until the crime scene was thoroughly searched and processed.

Today, the Borden house where the murders took place is a museum and a bed-and-breakfast where guests can spend the night. Some people believe the house is haunted.

The processing of the crime scene would also have been very different today. In 1892, detectives working the scene moved the victims' bodies, which could have tainted them. In particular, detectives moved Mrs. Borden's body before photographing. Then they attempted to place her body back in its original position for photographing. They later moved the bodies downstairs where they were placed on cooling boards on the dining room table. These boards allowed the bodies to cool faster and allowed bodily fluids to drain. The victims' stomachs were removed and sent to Harvard Medical School to be examined. Then Dr. Dolan took the bodies to the local undertaker. Nearly a week after the murders, Dolan performed an autopsy at the Oak Grove Cemetery.

Today, the entire crime scene would be photographed before anything was moved. The victims' bodies would be examined, and their hands would be covered in plastic to preserve any DNA evidence under their fingernails. Every piece of evidence would be documented, collected, and preserved.

LIZZIE'S LAST DAYS

Lizzie Borden was an intensely private woman. After her death in 1927, there was renewed interest in the 1892 murders. Lizzie's close friend Helen Leighton allowed herself to be interviewed by the press and painted a picture of Lizzie's state of mind in her final years. She said:

> *Miss Borden was bitterly unhappy. Tragedy and sorrow ever overshadowed her. Only on rare occasions did she lay aside the sorrows. These happy and gay moments usually seem[ed] to come when she was away from Fall River. . . . But these moments of happiness were fleeting. . . . I know in later years she questioned the wisdom of having remained in Fall River. . . . She wondered if it would not have been better had she settled in another place.*[3]

Crime scene investigators would spray chemicals such as luminol to reveal tiny amounts of blood that could not be seen with the naked eye. Ultraviolet light might be used to search for other biological evidence such as saliva. Every surface would be examined for fingerprints. Once the crime scene work was complete, the bodies would be sent to the medical examiner's office for autopsy and forensic testing.

An Enduring Mystery

The public's continued fascination with the Borden murders over the years has made Lizzie Borden a lasting part of pop culture. Her story has been told onstage in the 1954 ballet *Fall River Legend*, the 1965 opera *Lizzie Borden*, and the 2009 rock opera *Lizzie: The Musical*. The story has been featured on television several times, from the 1975 made-for-television movie *The Legend of Lizzie Borden* to the Lifetime Network's series called *The Lizzie Borden Chronicles*. Lizzie has even appeared on the big screen in 2018's *Lizzie*, starring Chloë Sevigny as Lizzie Borden and Kristen Stewart as Bridget Sullivan. In addition, Lizzie's story has inspired numerous books, podcasts, and documentaries.

Lizzie Borden and the murders for which she was accused remain a mystery. No one has ever been able to definitively prove whether she was involved in the crime. The murders of Andrew and Abby Borden remain unsolved. Many believe

Tourists visit the Borden house in Fall River.

A painting of Lizzie hangs in her family's Fall River home in 2008.

the jury of 12 men returned the correct verdict based on the evidence presented to them. However, just because

they decided that Lizzie was not guilty, does that mean she was innocent? The question remains.

TIMELINE

1860

- In July, Lizzie Andrew Borden is born.

1863

- In March, Lizzie's mother, Sarah Borden, dies.

1865

- In June, Lizzie's father, Andrew Borden, marries 37-year-old Abby Durfee Gray.

1892

- On August 2, Abby and Andrew Borden complain of nausea and stomach pains. Mrs. Borden visits a doctor and suggests she might have been poisoned, but the doctor says she probably just ate spoiled fish.
- On August 3, Lizzie reportedly attempts to buy prussic acid. The pharmacist refuses to sell it to her without a prescription. John Vinnicum Morse arrives at the Borden house for an unexpected visit.
- On August 4, Andrew and Abby Borden are found murdered in their home. The police search the house but do not notice anything out of place.

- On August 6, funeral services for Andrew and Abby Borden are held at the Borden home. The police search the home again.
- On August 7, Alice Russell sees Lizzie burning a light blue dress in the kitchen. When asked about it, Lizzie says that the dress is ruined with paint stains.
- Between August 9 and August 11, an inquest is held to gather more information about the murders of Andrew and Abby Borden. Lizzie's testimony is confused and contradictory.
- On August 11, Lizzie is arrested.
- On August 12, Lizzie enters a plea of not guilty.
- In December, a grand jury indicts Lizzie on murder charges.

1893

- On June 5, the trial of Lizzie Borden begins at the New Bedford Courthouse.
- On June 20, a jury declares Lizzie not guilty.

1927

- In June, Lizzie dies at age 67.

ESSENTIAL FACTS

SIGNIFICANT EVENTS

- On August 4, 1892, Andrew and Abby Borden are found murdered in their home, hacked to death with an ax or hatchet.
- On August 11, 1892, Lizzie Borden is arrested on suspicion of murdering her father and stepmother.
- On June 20, 1893, a jury decides Lizzie is not guilty. While many people welcome Lizzie back to her hometown, Fall River, the public's opinion soon turns against her. People believe she got away with murder.
- In 1927, Lizzie dies. Since her acquittal in court, no one else has ever been charged with the Borden murders. The case remains unsolved.

KEY PLAYERS

- Lizzie Borden was accused of killing her father and stepmother, Andrew and Abby Borden.
- Andrew and Abby Borden were killed on August 4, 1892. Mr. Borden was a successful businessman and the father of Lizzie and Emma Borden. Mrs. Borden had a strained relationship with her stepdaughters.
- Bridget Sullivan was the Bordens' housemaid. She and Lizzie were the only two people at the Borden house at the time of the murders.
- Hosea Knowlton, the district attorney for the Southern District of Massachusetts, was responsible for the investigation and prosecution of the Borden murders.
- Andrew Jennings, the Borden family lawyer, led Lizzie's defense team during her murder trial.

IMPACT ON SOCIETY

In the 1890s, the murders of Andrew and Abby Borden in their home in the middle of the day fascinated many people because of the violent and gruesome details of the case. When Lizzie Borden was arrested for the murders of her father and stepmother, her trial became one of the most sensational trials in American history. At the time, it was unheard of for a woman, let alone a woman of Borden's social status, to have committed a murder, especially as she was accused of violently hacking her own father and stepmother to death with an ax. Newspapers and magazines sensationalized the murder trial and stirred the public's interest in the case. Despite the best efforts of the police, Lizzie Borden was acquitted, and the crime was never solved. The case has been the inspiration for many theories, as well as a number of books, movies, and documentaries. Through it all, the question remains—did the jury get it wrong? Was Lizzie Borden guilty?

QUOTE

"The Borden case is without parallel in the criminal history of America. It is the most interesting and perhaps the most puzzling murder which has occurred in this country."

—*Edmund Lester Pearson, true crime writer, in 1924, three years before Lizzie's death*

GLOSSARY

acquitted
Found not guilty of a criminal act.

autopsy
The examination of a body after death to determine the cause of death.

buggy
A light one-horse carriage used for transportation.

calico
A type of cotton fabric.

civil engineer
A person who works with construction designs, particularly related to public works such as roads or bridges.

cordial
Warm and friendly.

editorial
An opinion essay by the editor of a publication.

eulogy
A personalized reading at a funeral to honor the deceased person.

frugal
Responsible and careful when spending money; not spending a lot of money.

hatchet
A small ax with a short handle for use in one hand.

laborer
A person whose job involves physical work.

marshal
A high-ranking law enforcement official.

medical examiner
An official trained in pathology who investigates deaths that occur under unusual or suspicious circumstances; sometimes called a coroner.

prosecution
Conducting legal proceedings against someone accused of a crime.

seamstress
A woman whose job is sewing.

suspect
A person thought to have committed a crime.

tenant
A person or business who rents from a landlord.

undertaker
A person who prepares for and manages funerals and burials.

ADDITIONAL RESOURCES

SELECTED BIBLIOGRAPHY

"Inquest Testimony of Lizzie Borden – August 9-11, Fall River Court Building," *Famous Trials*, n.d., famous-trials.com. Accessed 26 Apr. 2019.

Martins, Michael, and Dennis A. Binette. *Parallel Lives: A Social History of Lizzie A. Borden and Her Fall River.* Fall River Historical Society, 2011.

Robertson, Cara. *The Trial of Lizzie Borden*. Simon & Schuster, 2019.

"Trial of Lizzie Andrew Borden 1893 Part One," *Lizzie Andrew Borden Virtual Museum & Library*, n.d., lizzieandrewborden.com. Accessed 27 Apr. 2019.

"Trial of Lizzie Andrew Borden 1893 Part Two," *Lizzie Andrew Borden Virtual Museum & Library*, n.d., lizzieandrewborden.com. Accessed 26 Apr. 2019.

FURTHER READINGS

Axelrod-Contrada, Joan. *The Lizzie Borden Axe Murder Trial: A Headline Court Case.* Enslow, 2000.

Burgan, Michael. *Lizzie Borden*. Aladdin, 2018.

Ius, Dawn. *Lizzie*. Simon Pulse, 2018.

Miller, Sarah Elizabeth. *The Borden Murders: Lizzie Borden and the Trial of the Century.* Schwartz & Wade Books, 2016.

ONLINE RESOURCES

To learn more about the Lizzie Borden ax murders, please visit **abdobooklinks.com** or scan this QR code. These links are routinely monitored and updated to provide the most current information available.

MORE INFORMATION

For more information on this subject, contact or visit the following organizations:

FALL RIVER HISTORICAL SOCIETY

451 Rock Street
Fall River, MA 02720
508-679-1071
lizzieborden.org

The Fall River Historical Society is dedicated to preserving the history of Fall River and sharing it with the public. It has an extensive collection of materials related to Lizzie Borden.

LIZZIE BORDEN BED AND BREAKFAST MUSEUM

230 Second Street
Fall River, MA 02721
508-675-7333
lizzie-borden.com

Visitors can tour and even spend the night in the Borden home where the murders occurred.

TOWN OF FALL RIVER

One Government Center
Fall River, MA 02722
508-324-2000
fallriverma.org

The visitor section of the Fall River, Massachusetts, website has information about visiting the town where Lizzie Borden lived, including the Oak Grove Cemetery where the Borden family is buried.

SOURCE NOTES

CHAPTER 1. A HORRIFYING CRIME

1. "Testimony of Bridget Sullivan in the Trial of Lizzie Borden." *Famous Trials*, 7 June 1893, famous-trials.com. Accessed 31 Mar. 2019.

2. "Testimony of Bridget Sullivan in the Trial of Lizzie Borden."

3. "Testimony of Adelaide B. Churchill in the Trial of Lizzie Borden," *Famous Trials*, 8 June 1893, famous-trials.com. Accessed 31 Mar. 2019.

4. "Testimony of Adelaide B. Churchill in the Trial of Lizzie Borden."

5. Fall River Herald. "Shocking Crime." *Famous Trials*, n.d., famous-trials.com. Accessed 31 Mar. 2019.

6. Paul Davis. "Testimony in Borden Trail Lacked Murder Weapon." *Daily Republic*, 3 July 2013, dailyrepublic.com. Accessed 31 Mar. 2019.

7. "The Witness Statements." *Lizzie Andrew Borden Virtual Museum & Library*, 6 Oct. 1892, lizzieandrewborden.com. Accessed 31 Mar. 2019.

8. Michael Martins and Dennis A. Binette. *Parallel Lives: A Social History of Lizzie A. Borden and Her Fall River*. Fall River Historical Society, 2011. 33.

CHAPTER 2. A WELL-KNOWN FAMILY

1. Paul Davis. "Fortunes of Lizzie Borden's Father Grew with Fall River." *Providence Journal*, 22 June 2013, providencejournal.com. Accessed 31 Mar. 2019.

2. Davis, "Fortunes of Lizzie Borden's Father Grew with Fall River."

3. "Population of the 100 Largest Urban Places." *U.S. Bureau of the Census*, 15 June 1998, census.gov. Accessed 19 Aug. 2019.

4. Cara Robertson. *The Trial of Lizzie Borden*. Simon & Schuster, 2019. 246–247.

CHAPTER 3. THE INVESTIGATION

1. Cara Robertson. *The Trial of Lizzie Borden*. Simon & Schuster, 2019. 503.

2. Robertson, *The Trial of Lizzie Borden*, 514.

3. "The Trial of Lizzie Borden: Autopsies." *Famous Trials*, n.d., famous-trials.com. Accessed 27 Apr. 2019.

CHAPTER 4. THE INQUEST

1. "Inquest Testimony of Lizzie Borden – August 9-11, Fall River Court Building," *Famous Trials*, n.d., famous-trials.com. Accessed 26 Apr. 2019.

2. "Inquest Testimony of Lizzie Borden – August 9-11, Fall River Court Building."

3. "Inquest Testimony of Lizzie Borden – August 9-11, Fall River Court Building."

4. Cara Robertson. *The Trial of Lizzie Borden*. Simon & Schuster, 2019. 53.

CHAPTER 5. THE ARREST

1. Sacramento Daily Union. "Lizzie Borden Arraigned." *UCR Center for Bibliographical Studies and Research*, 9 May 1893, cdnc.ucr.edu. Accessed 19 Aug. 2019.

2. Harry Widdows. "Crime in the City: Fall River, 1892." *Lizzie Andrew Borden Virtual Museum & Library*, 14 July 2018, lizzieandrewborden.com. Accessed 19 Aug. 2019.

3. Michael Martins and Dennis A. Binette. *Parallel Lives: A Social History of Lizzie A. Borden and Her Fall River*. Fall River Historical Society, 2011. 472.

4. Cara Robertson. *The Trial of Lizzie Borden*. Simon & Schuster, 2019. 898.

5. Robertson, *The Trial of Lizzie Borden*, 1003.

6. Robertson, *The Trial of Lizzie Borden*, 62.

7. Robertson, *The Trial of Lizzie Borden*, 1136.

8. Caitlyn Walters. "Rumors, Lies and Alibis: How Newspapers Sensationalized the Lizzie Borden Murder Case, August 1892- June 1893." *Atlanta Review of Journalism History*, vol. 11, no. 1, 2014. academia.edu. Accessed 19 Aug. 2019.

9. "Trial of Lizzie Andrew Borden 1893 Part One," *Lizzie Andrew Borden Virtual Museum & Library*, n.d., lizzieandrewborden.com. Accessed 27 Apr. 2019.

SOURCE NOTES CONTINUED

CHAPTER 6. THE PROSECUTION'S CASE

1. Cara Robertson. *The Trial of Lizzie Borden*. Simon & Schuster, 2019. 1485.

2. Robertson, *The Trial of Lizzie Borden*, 1557–1558.

3. "Trial of Lizzie Andrew Borden 1893 Part Two," *Lizzie Andrew Borden Virtual Museum & Library*, n.d., lizzieandrewborden.com. Accessed 26 Apr. 2019.

4. "Trial of Lizzie Andrew Borden 1893 Part Two."

5. "Trial of Lizzie Andrew Borden 1893 Part Two."

6. "Trial of Lizzie Andrew Borden 1893 Part Two."

CHAPTER 7. LIZZIE BORDEN'S DEFENSE

1. "Trial of Lizzie Andrew Borden 1893 Part Two," *Lizzie Andrew Borden Virtual Museum & Library*, n.d., lizzieandrewborden.com. Accessed 26 Apr. 2019.

2. "Trial of Lizzie Andrew Borden 1893 Part Two."

3. "Trial of Lizzie Andrew Borden 1893 Part Two."

4. Edwin H. Porter. *The Fall River Tragedy: A History of the Borden Murders*. Lawbook Exchange, 2006. 85.

5. "Trial of Lizzie Andrew Borden 1893 Part Two."

6. Michael Martins and Dennis A. Binette. *Parallel Lives: A Social History of Lizzie A. Borden and Her Fall River*. Fall River Historical Society, 2011. 487.

7. "Trial of Lizzie Andrew Borden 1893 Part Two."

8. "Trial of Lizzie Andrew Borden 1893 Part Two."

CHAPTER 8. THE VERDICT

1. "Trial of Lizzie Andrew Borden 1893 Part Two," *Lizzie Andrew Borden Virtual Museum & Library*, n.d., lizzieandrewborden.com. Accessed 26 Apr. 2019.

2. "Trial of Lizzie Andrew Borden 1893 Part Two."

3. "Trial of Lizzie Andrew Borden 1893 Part Two."

4. "Trial of Lizzie Andrew Borden 1893 Part Two."

5. Cara Robertson. *The Trial of Lizzie Borden*. Simon & Schuster, 2019. 4039.

6. "The Acquittal of Miss Borden," *New York Times*, 21 June 1893, nytimes.com. Accessed 19 Aug. 2019.

7. "The Acquittal of Miss Borden."

CHAPTER 9. WHO KILLED THE BORDENS?

1. Cara Robertson. *The Trial of Lizzie Borden*. Simon & Schuster, 2019. 4125.

2. Michael Martins and Dennis A. Binette. *Parallel Lives: A Social History of Lizzie A. Borden and Her Fall River*. Fall River Historical Society, 2011. 988–989.

3. Martins and Binette, *Parallel Lives: A Social History of Lizzie A. Borden and Her Fall River*, 992.

INDEX

ABOUT THE AUTHOR

Carla Mooney is a graduate of the University of Pennsylvania. Today, she writes for young people and is the author of many books for young adults and children. Mooney enjoys reading about true crime and investigations.